D0188304

THE BEST

GLUTEN-FREE, WHEAT-FREE & DAIRY-FREE RECIPES

THE BEST GLUTEN-FREE, WHEAT-FREE & DAIRY-FREE RECIPES

MORE THAN 100 MOUTH-WATERING RECIPES FOR ALL THE FAMILY

GRACE CHEETHAM

DUNCAN BAIRD PUBLISHERS

LONDON

The Best Gluten-Free, Wheat-Free
& Dairy-Free Recipes
Grace Cheetham

First published in the United Kingdom
and Ireland in 2007 by
Duncan Baird Publishers Ltd
Sixth Floor, Castle House
75–76 Wells Street, London W1T 3QH

Conceived, created and designed by
Duncan Baird Publishers

Editor: Alison Bolus
Managing Designer: Daniel Sturges
Commissioned photography: William Lingwood
Food stylists: Lucy McKelvie, Fergal Connolly
and Martha Dunkerley
Prop stylist: Helen Trent

British Library Cataloguing-in-Publication Data:
A CIP record for this book is available from the
British Library

ISBN: 978-1-84483-456-3

10 9 8 7 6 5 4 3 2 1

Typeset in Helvetica
Colour reproduction by Scanhouse, Malaysia
Printed in China by Imago

For Peter

Publisher's note: While every care has been taken in compiling the recipes for this book, Duncan Baird Publishers, or any other persons who have been involved in working on this publication, cannot accept responsibility for any errors or omissions, inadvertent or not, that may be found in the recipes or text, or for any problems that may arise as a result of preparing one of these recipes. It is important that you consult a medical professional before following any of the recipes or information contained in this book if you have any special dietary requirements or medical conditions. Ill or elderly people, babies, young children and women who are pregnant or breastfeeding should avoid the recipes containing raw meat or uncooked eggs.

Notes on the recipes

- Use organic ingredients
- Use fresh, unsweetened soya milk
- Do not mix metric and imperial measurements
- 1 tsp = 5ml   1 tbsp = 15ml   1 cup = 250ml

Unless otherwise stated:

- Use medium fruit, vegetables and eggs
- Use fresh herbs

Notes on the symbols

The food symbols refer to the recipes only, not to any serving suggestions. They are used even when only a small amount of an item is present, such as sugar in fish sauce, salt in tamari soy sauce, yeast in vinegar and seeds in sesame and rapeseed oils. Peanuts have been classed as nuts and pine nuts as seeds. Also, date syrup, honey and molasses have been classed as sugars because they have a similar effect on blood sugar levels to sugar, but the sugar symbol hasn't been used for wine, as the varieties vary so significantly. A few of the recipes contain gluten: these are clearly marked with the gluten symbol. Check the manufacturer's labelling carefully before using any food or drink, since the ingredients used by different brands do vary, especially regarding small quantities of ingredients such as salt, sugar or oil, although be aware that manufacturers are not required to detail minuscule quantities of ingredients.

contents

KEY TO SYMBOLS

 contains gluten

 contains yeast

 contains eggs

 contains nuts

 contains seeds

 contains salt

 contains sugar

introduction

Embarking on a restricted diet can seem so hard. Often the foods you have to cut out of your diet are the ones you crave and think you can't live without. You think your meals will be difficult to prepare, and boring. But this book will show you how deliciously easy to prepare – and truly enjoyable – they can be. Packed full of mouth-watering recipes, all simple to make, it'll show you how to create fantastic food for your daily life. Here are meals to enjoy at home with your family and friends, or to pack up and take with you. Flick through these pages and you'll find a delicious selection of breakfasts, lunches, teas and snacks, dinners, sides and desserts. From biscuits and brownies to crêpes and cupcakes, from spaghetti and sushi to pasta and pizza, they're all here – and all specifically designed to suit your diet.

In the beginning

When I was first diagnosed with an intolerance to gluten, wheat and dairy, I was devastated. I remember my father took me to a café after I had seen the doctor, and we stared at the menu in complete confusion. I couldn't have any of the breads, cakes or biscuits or any of my favourite drinks. In the end I ordered a glass of apple juice and sat there miserably. And for a long time my culinary experiences were like this – a mixture of bewilderment and despair. Gradually, I became used to going without, although my diet was bland, boring and very restricted. But over the years I started to experiment with cooking, learning to make meals that were naturally gluten-, wheat- and dairy-free, and I worked out ones that I could not only eat at home but also take with me for the day, if necessary. I also started to try out different products from health-food stores, delicatessens and supermarkets: dairy-free milks, margarines and cheeses, different flours and grains, and new flavourings or sauces. Eating became less of the flavourless rice cakes and more of the delicious breads, pizzas, biscuits, cakes and desserts that you'll find here.

I've put the best of these recipes into this book, in the hope that you will find many that you love. There's a range of recipes using alternative ingredients instead of gluten, wheat or dairy, as well as recipes that are naturally free of these ingredients. Here are breakfasts ranging from vitamin-packed smoothies to sustaining hot dishes; lunches to take with you or to enjoy at home; teas and snacks for when you want to treat yourself; dinners, including simple suppers you can whip up in minutes, family meals you'll all love and indulgent feasts, with side dishes; and desserts for when you're feeling decadent. Mix and match to suit yourself – eat Blueberry and Banana Muffins for tea, for example, rather than breakfast, nibble on Apricot, Mango and Coconut Bars for breakfast, instead of later on, or have a blow-out lunch with any of the dinner recipes, such as Duck with Cherry and Juniper Sauce or Gnocchi with Mushroom and Pancetta Sauce. It's up to you!

Spinach Tart (see page 76)

Smoked Salmon, Prawn and Vegetable Sushi (see page 65)

Following a gluten-free, wheat-free and/or dairy-free diet

Getting your head around and following a restrictive diet is hard. It can seem so very tiring, monotonous and isolating. At first, the idea of having to prepare every single meal yourself feels utterly daunting. You long to be able to pick up a take-away pizza or a sandwich from a deli and to share your family's or friends' food. But the benefits of sticking to your diet are so great that they do make it all worthwhile. I've written this book in the hope that I'll be able to make it easy for you. I've purposely made all the recipes simple to follow and use. Many of them can be cooked in under half an hour – and some can be pulled together in minutes. Don't be alarmed by the prospect of making sushi, pizza or bread, because you'll find that they're all remarkably do-able, and I've often included short-cut methods, including using a food processor method for whizzing together pastry, cakes or desserts. All the ingredients are easy to obtain, and all the recipes have symbols for immediate reference showing whether they contain gluten, yeast, eggs, nuts, seeds, salt or sugar, even if it's only a small amount. For people who can eat gluten but not wheat, I've included a few recipes with gluten, but these are marked with the gluten symbol. You won't need a vast array of kitchen equipment to make this food, or great culinary expertise. What's more, these are delicious recipes that you can share with your family or friends – from normal, everyday lunches to smart dinners and extravagant meals for special occasions.

On the plus side

One of the great benefits of following a diet such as this is that you are likely to eat far more healthily. By taking gluten, wheat and dairy out of your diet, you will be forced to abandon much of the junk food available and to eat fresher, purer, more nutritious produce, which can only be a good thing. When your body reacts to the foods to which it is allergic or intolerant, it can go into defence mode, and can cause a range of symptoms including

nausea, vomiting, headaches, migraines, rashes, eczema, asthma attacks, anaphylactic shock, bloating, bowel problems, chronic fatigue and depression. Your body can then counteract by producing extra adrenaline to fight the reaction and, in doing so, compromises your immune system. So, apart from avoiding the problem foods, the best thing you can do for your body is to build up your reserves of vitamins, minerals and other essential nutrients, and generally support your immune system as much as possible.

While you can buy a good variety of foods specially adapted for this kind of diet, they often contain additives and preservatives, which can be damaging, and often have very little nutritional value. In contrast, I've used a lot of fresh fruit and vegetables throughout this book as well as essential fatty-acid-rich oils and fructose instead of high-GI (glycaemic index) sugar. I've also used less salt and fructose than normal. The Confit of Duck, for example, uses only a quarter of the normal amount of salt, and the cakes and desserts, particularly the chocolate ones, do not have the sickly-sweet taste of often over-sugared ready-made produce. By cooking the meals on the following pages, you can not only make a positive effect on your health and well-being by following your diet properly but also benefit greatly from the nutritional excellence of healthy home-cooking.

Getting started

The first thing to do is to ensure that you have a basic collection of pans, dishes and tins, some scales or a set of cup measures, some measuring spoons and possibly a food processor and/or a hand-held electric blender/whisk. Then stock your storecupboard – either just a few ingredients at a time or by going on a full-on shopping spree, which will mean you'll have all the basics to hand and great snacks and bites to munch on whenever you feel hungry.

(*opposite*) Raspberry Tarts (see page 91)

Instead of flours containing gluten, I've used a variety of flours throughout the recipes. Rice flour and gram (or chickpea) flour are great alternatives in muffins, cakes, biscuits, breads and pastry, and have a lovely subtle taste. Maize flour (a finer-milled version of polenta) has a more granular texture and a slightly sweeter flavour, and potato flour and millet flour are useful as fillers or thickeners. Very occasionally, I've used a couple of flours that contain gluten: barley flour has excellent binding properties, but I've used it in only small amounts as the taste can be overpowering, and the classic rye flour is great for flavour and texture. If you can't tolerate gluten, you can use the gluten-free alternatives given in many of the recipes, and substitute one of the other breads for the rye bread.

There is now a fantastic selection of dairy-free products available. I've used soya milk throughout the recipes and highly recommend the fresh, sugar-free versions as they taste much better than the longlife kinds and last for a considerable amount of time in the fridge. If you like, you could always use goats' or sheep's milk instead (if you can tolerate them), or rice, oat (if you can tolerate gluten) or any of the nut milks otherwise. I've also used soya yogurt and soya cheeses (again, you could substitute goats' or sheep's), tofu and soya margarines, which you could substitute with any of the dairy-free olive oil spreads.

I've used olive oil throughout because it's easy to obtain and is also a very stable oil that can be heated to a high heat without any problems. But you could easily use rapeseed at high temperatures, or any of the other nutritious oils such as safflower or soya bean oil, if you're not heating them to high temperatures, or hemp seed or flaxseed oil for salads.

I've also used fruit sugar, or fructose, which is basically unrefined sugar from fruit. This is a great alternative to normal refined sugar as it has a GI level five times lower than sucrose. I've also used date syrup as it also has a low GI score and contains valuable nutrients.

It's well worth stocking up on dried fruits, and nuts and seeds as they can make all the difference to a recipe, as well as being great snack foods. Almonds and coconuts, in particular, are gems: they are packed with nutrients and utterly delicious, but are also great to bake with and to use in various forms to add a rich, intense flavour.

Stock up, too, on essences, spices and other flavourings, such as tamari (a wheat-free soy sauce) and gluten-, yeast- and dairy-free stock powder. Pulses and beans are also fantastically useful: they can add inexpensive, comforting substance to any recipe, and are a great source of protein and fibre, as well as being low GI. Try haricot beans, butter beans, Puy lentils, chickpeas – the list goes on and on. Finally, fill your cupboards with polenta, rices (basmati, risotto and whole-grain in particular), rice paper sheets and noodles, gluten-free and wheat-free pastas and noodles, and different types of flakes such as oat, barley, rice, buckwheat, amaranth and quinoa, and you'll have the base for all types of meals.

Sign up to an organic delivery scheme and enjoy the benefits of fresh, locally grown fruit and vegetables, meat, fish and other basics, without the hassle of shopping or carting heavy bags home. It is vital that you avoid the added chemicals in non-organic food, particularly meat and fish, and eating organic food also enables you to eat more in tune with the seasons, bringing you nearer to the natural state of food that enriches our bodies. Try to eat as many salads, steamed and raw vegetables and fruit as possible, as these will support your immune system immensely, to make additives and preservatives (which can have unpleasant side effects) a thing of the past and to drink lots of clean, pure water.

Further help

Consult a nutritionist or naturopath, who will help you to identify any other problem foods as well as advise you on health-enhancing supplements. Spoil yourself by indulging in complementary therapies such as massage, acupuncture, healing – whatever helps you to find calm and happiness. But, above all, stick with the diet: you're bound to notice the benefits of reduced symptoms as well as greatly enhanced health and vitality. Go for it!

basics

Use this chapter for all the basic recipes you'll need. Whether it's a simple stock or pastry recipe, for example, or a fresh Tomato and Pepper Sauce, a rich Hollandaise Sauce or a fiery Thai Green Curry Paste, they're all here. You'll also find various bread recipes, all of which are easy to make and useful for every day: to eat for breakfast, with soups, salads or pâtés, or whenever hunger hits and you need a filling snack. You'll find that many of the recipes work slightly differently from standard ones that use gluten, wheat and dairy, due to the nature of the ingredients used here. But don't worry – they do work! And once you've baked your own Soda Bread, whipped up a Salmon and Prawn Fish Pie with Béchamel Sauce, or a Tarte Tatin with gluten-free pastry, there'll be no looking back!

tomato and pepper sauce

Makes about 1.2 litres/2 pints/5 cups.

1 Preheat the grill to high. Cut 3 red, orange or yellow peppers (or a mixture of colours) in half lengthways and remove the seeds and pith. Place, cut-side down, on a grill rack and cook under the hot grill for 4–5 minutes until the skins are black. Put into a plastic food bag and leave for 2–3 minutes. Remove from the bag, peel off the skins and cut the flesh into chunks.

2 Meanwhile, with a sharp knife, cut a cross in the skins of 1.5kg/3lb 5oz vine-ripened tomatoes, place in a large, heatproof bowl and cover with boiling water. Leave to stand for 2–3 minutes, then remove from the water, peel off the skins and chop coarsely.

3 Heat 2 tbsp olive oil in a heavy-based saucepan over a low heat. Add 1 finely chopped large onion and cook for 2–3 minutes until it begins to turn golden. Add 2 crushed garlic cloves and cook for 30 seconds, then stir in 1 tbsp tomato purée, the peppers and tomatoes.

4 Turn the heat up to medium and cook for 15–20 minutes until the sauce has thickened and reduced. Season lightly with sea salt and freshly ground black pepper.

béchamel sauce

Makes about 650ml/22fl oz/2⅔ cups.

1 Place 175ml/6fl oz/¾ cup sugar-free soya milk, 1 chopped onion, ½ chopped leek and 2 bay leaves in a saucepan. Bring to the boil, then turn the heat down, cover with a lid and leave to simmer for 3–4 minutes. Remove from the heat and leave to infuse for 20 minutes.

2 Melt 50g/2oz dairy-free margarine in a heavy-based saucepan over a low heat. Stir in 40g/1¾oz/heaped ⅓ cup gram flour and 40g/1¾oz/scant ¼ cup rice flour. Remove the pan from the heat.

3 Gradually stir in 450ml/¾ pint/1¾ cups Vegetable Stock (see page 25), or stock made with gluten-, yeast- and dairy-free stock powder, then the infused milk, stirring all the time.

4 Return the pan to the heat and bring to the boil, stirring continuously as it thickens. It it goes lumpy, beat with a whisk until it is smooth again.

5 Once the sauce has boiled, turn the heat down and let it simmer very gently for 10 minutes. Stir frequently to prevent it sticking to the pan. Stir in another ½–1 cup stock to make a smooth sauce that is thick, but still runny. Season lightly with sea salt and freshly ground black pepper.

white wine sauce

Makes about 550ml/19fl oz/2¼ cups.

1 Melt 25g/1oz dairy-free margarine in a heavy-based saucepan over a low heat. Stir in 35g/1½oz/⅓ cup gram flour and 3 tbsp rice flour. Remove the pan from the heat.

2 Gradually stir in 125ml/4fl oz/½ cup organic dry white wine, 85ml/3fl oz/⅓ cup sugar-free soya milk and 200ml/7fl oz/¾ cup Vegetable Stock (see page 25), or stock made with gluten-, yeast- and dairy-free stock powder, stirring the sauce all the time.

3 Return the pan to the heat and bring to the boil, stirring continuously as it thickens. It it goes lumpy, beat with a whisk until it is smooth again.

4 Once the sauce has boiled, turn the heat down and let it simmer very gently for 10 minutes. Stir frequently to prevent it sticking to the pan. Stir in another ½–1 cup stock to make a smooth sauce that is thick, but still runny. Season lightly with sea salt and freshly ground black pepper.

hollandaise sauce

Makes about 300ml/10fl oz/1⅓ cups.

1 Pour 2 tbsp white wine vinegar and 2 tbsp water into a small saucepan and add 1 tsp ground white pepper. Bring to the boil, then turn the heat down and leave to simmer for 2–3 minutes until the liquid has reduced by half. Tip into a shallow bowl and leave until cold.

2 Place 4 egg yolks in a heatproof bowl and beat. Gradually whisk in the cold vinegar mixture, a little at a time, until thoroughly mixed in.

3 Place the bowl over a saucepan of gently simmering water, so that the bowl rests on the rim of the pan and does not touch the water. Keep whisking the mixture in the bowl for 3–4 minutes until it is as thick as you can get it.

4 Cut 100g/3½oz dairy-free margarine into small pieces and add a little at a time, whisking constantly.

5 Pour in 1 tbsp lemon juice and quickly whisk again to mix in, taking care not to overheat, as the sauce will curdle. Season lightly with sea salt and ground white pepper and serve immediately.

ras el hanout

Makes about 4 tbsp.

1 Heat a heavy-based frying pan over a low heat. Add 1 tsp each cumin seeds and coriander seeds and dry-fry for 2–3 minutes until they start to brown. Keep the seeds moving all the time so they do not burn.

2 Remove from the heat and grind to a fine powder using a pestle and mortar or electric hand-held mini blender. Place in a small bowl.

3 Add 2 tsp each sweet smoked paprika and ground ginger, 1 tsp each turmeric and ground cinnamon and ½ tsp each cayenne pepper, freshly grated nutmeg, ground cloves, ground allspice, sea salt and freshly ground black pepper.

4 Stir well to mix together, then transfer to a clean storage jar with a tight-fitting lid. Keep in a cool, dark place for 5–6 months and use as required.

thai green curry paste

Makes about 12 tbsp.

1 Heat a heavy-based frying pan over a low heat. Add ½ tbsp each cumin seeds and coriander seeds and dry-fry for 2–3 minutes until they start to brown. Keep the seeds moving all the time so they do not burn.

2 Remove from the heat and grind to a fine powder using a pestle and mortar or electric hand-held mini blender. Place in a liquidizer or food processor.

3 Peel and coarsely chop the bottom half of 2 lemongrass stalks and add, along with 6 deseeded and coarsely chopped large green chillies, 4 chopped shallots, a 2cm/¾in piece fresh ginger, peeled and chopped, and 4 chopped garlic cloves. Blend well.

4 Add 2 tsp shrimp paste, 5 chopped kaffir lime leaves (or a strip of lime peel) and 6 chopped coriander stems with roots and leaves, or 1 small handful coarsely chopped coriander leaves and stems, and blend to form a coarse paste. Put in an airtight container and store in the fridge for up to 1 week.

rich shortcrust pastry

1 Sift 85g/3oz/scant $^{1}/_{2}$ cup rice flour, 85g/3oz/heaped $^{3}/_{4}$ cup gram flour, 30g/1$^{1}/_{4}$oz/$^{1}/_{3}$ cup barley flour and $^{1}/_{2}$ tsp sea salt into a large mixing bowl. Cut 125g/4oz chilled dairy-free margarine into small cubes and, using cold fingertips, rub it into the flours until the mixture resembles fine breadcrumbs.

2 Make a well in the centre and add 1 beaten large egg, mixing lightly with a round-bladed knife so that the mixture begins to hold together. It needs to form a dough with a little extra moisture at the base of the bowl. If it is too dry, gradually add 1–2 tbsp chilled water to make it quite sticky. If too sticky, add some rice flour.

3 Shape the pastry into a ball. Wrap in greaseproof paper and put in the fridge for 30 minutes. This amount will line a 25cm/10in tart tin, 3cm/1$^{1}/_{4}$in deep, or 5 x 12cm/5in tartlet tins, 2cm/$^{3}/_{4}$in deep.

4 The pastry can also be made in a food processor. Simply tip the sifted flours and salt into the bowl, add the margarine and blend until the mixture resembles fine breadcrumbs. Add the egg and blend for 20–30 seconds until the mixture comes together to form a sticky dough, adding more water if needed.

rich shortcrust pastry (gluten-free)

1 Sift 85g/3oz/scant $^{1}/_{2}$ cup rice flour, 85g/3oz/heaped $^{3}/_{4}$ cup gram flour, 30g/1$^{1}/_{4}$oz/$^{1}/_{4}$ cup buckwheat flour and $^{1}/_{2}$ tsp sea salt into a large mixing bowl. Cut 125g/4oz chilled dairy-free margarine into small cubes and, using cold fingertips, rub it into the flours until the mixture resembles fine breadcrumbs.

2 Make a well in the centre and add 1 beaten large egg, mixing lightly with a round-bladed knife so that the mixture begins to hold together. It needs to form a dough with a little extra moisture at the base of the bowl. If it is too dry, gradually add 1–2 tbsp chilled water to make it quite sticky. If too sticky, add some rice flour.

3 Shape the pastry into a ball. Wrap in greaseproof paper and put in the fridge for 30 minutes. This amount will line a 25cm/10in tart tin, 3cm/1$^{1}/_{4}$in deep, or 5 x 12cm/5in tartlet tins, 2cm/$^{3}/_{4}$in deep.

4 The pastry can also be made in a food processor (see Rich Shortcrust Pastry).

5 Note that this pastry is very fragile and needs to be handled with great care. Roll it out quickly and smoothly, use a board to turn it into the tin and use your fingertips to mould the pastry together if it cracks a little when you turn it into the tin.

sweet rich shortcrust pastry

1. Sift 75g/2½oz/scant ½ cup rice flour and 75g/2½oz/⅔ cup gram flour into a large mixing bowl. Stir in 50g/2oz/scant ½ cup ground almonds and 35g/1½oz/scant ¼ cup fruit sugar. Cut 80g/2¾ oz chilled dairy-free margarine into small cubes and, using cold fingertips, rub it into the dry ingredients until the mixture resembles fine breadcrumbs.
2. Make a well in the centre and add 1 beaten large egg, mixing lightly with a round-bladed knife so that the mixture begins to hold together. It needs to form a dough with a little extra moisture at the base of the bowl. If it is too dry, gradually add 1–2 tbsp chilled water to make it quite sticky. If too sticky, add some rice flour.
3. Shape the pastry into a ball. Wrap in greaseproof paper and put in the fridge for 30 minutes. This amount will line a 25cm/10in tart tin, 3cm/1¼in deep, or 5 x 12cm/5in tartlet tins, 2cm/¾in deep.
4. The pastry can also be made in a food processor (see Rich Shortcrust Pastry), adding the ground almonds and sugar with the sifted flours.

tarte tatin pastry

1. Sift 75g/2½oz/scant ½ cup rice flour, 50g/2oz/scant ½ cup gram flour and 50g/2oz/scant ½ cup ground almonds into a large mixing bowl and stir in 50g/2oz/⅓ cup fruit sugar. Cut 75g/2½oz chilled dairy-free margarine into small pieces and, using cold fingertips, rub it into the dry ingredients until the mixture resembles fine breadcrumbs.
2. Make a well in the centre and add 1 beaten large egg, mixing lightly with a round-bladed knife so that the mixture begins to hold together. Continue adding the egg gradually until it is all mixed in and the mixture begins to come together to form a sticky dough.
3. Shape the pastry into a ball. Wrap in greaseproof paper and put in the fridge for at least 30 minutes. This amount will line a 25cm/10in tart tin, 3cm/1¼in deep, or 5 x 12cm/5in tartlet tins, 2cm/¾in deep.
4. The pastry can also be made in a food processor (see Rich Shortcrust Pastry), adding the ground almonds and sugar with the sifted flours.

rye bread

1 Crumble 25g/1oz fresh yeast, if using, into 250ml/9fl oz/1 cup warm water and leave to prove (go frothy) for 10 minutes.
2 Sift 300g/10oz/3 cups rye flour, 85g/3oz/ scant $^1/_2$ cup rice flour, 85g/3oz/heaped $^3/_4$ cup gram flour, 30g/1$^1/_4$oz/ $^1/_3$ cup barley flour, 90g/3$^1/_4$oz/$^2/_3$ cup pumpkin seeds and $^1/_2$ tsp salt into a large mixing bowl. If not using fresh yeast, add a 7g/ $^1/_4$oz sachet easy-blend dried yeast.
3 Make a well in the centre and pour in 2 tbsp date syrup and the proved yeast, if using. Gradually draw the flour into the liquid using a wooden spoon, mixing well to form a soft dough. If it feels dry, add extra water 1 tbsp at a time; if sticky, add rye flour.
4 Turn the dough out onto a surface dusted with rye flour and knead for 10 minutes until smooth and elastic. Return to the bowl, cover with a damp tea towel and leave until doubled in size – about 1 hour.
5 Lightly grease a baking tray with dairy-free margarine. Turn the dough out and knead for 2 minutes. Shape into a loaf and place on the baking tray. Cover and leave to rise for 45–60 minutes. Preheat the oven to 200°C/400°F/Gas 6.
6 Bake for 35–40 minutes until it is brown on top and sounds hollow when tapped on the base. Transfer to a wire rack to cool.

soda bread

1 Preheat the oven to 200°C/400°F/Gas 6. Lightly grease a baking tray with dairy-free margarine. Sift 80g/2$^3/_4$oz/ $^1/_2$ cup potato flour, 60g/2$^1/_4$oz/heaped $^1/_2$ cup gram flour and 150g/5oz/scant 1 cup rice flour into a large mixing bowl and stir in $^1/_2$ tsp salt and 1 tsp bicarbonate of soda. Cut 25g/1oz chilled dairy-free margarine into small cubes and, using cold fingertips, rub it into the flours until the mixture resembles fine breadcrumbs.
2 Make a well in the centre and pour in 1 beaten large egg and 125ml/4fl oz/ $^1/_2$ cup sugar-free soya milk. Mix well with a wooden spoon until all the ingredients are well combined, then bring together with your hands to form a ball of dough.
3 Turn the dough out onto a surface dusted with rice flour and knead briefly, ensuring there are no lumps. Shape into a flattened round and place on the prepared baking tray. Cut a cross about 1cm/ $^1/_2$in deep on the top.
4 Bake in the hot oven for 30–35 minutes until it is lightly browned and risen and sounds hollow when tapped on the base. Transfer to a wire rack and leave to cool completely before serving.

corn bread

1 Preheat the oven to 200°C/400°F/Gas 6. Lightly grease a 450g/1lb loaf tin with dairy-free margarine.

2 Sift 150g/5oz/1 cup maize flour and 150g/5oz/1 cup rice flour into a large mixing bowl and stir in 1 tsp gluten-free baking powder and 1 tsp salt. Cut 50g/2oz chilled dairy-free margarine into small pieces and, using cold fingertips, rub it into the flour until the mixture resembles breadcrumbs.

3 In a small bowl, beat 2 large eggs and mix in 300ml/10fl oz/1¼ cups sugar-free soya milk. Make a well in the centre of the flour mixture and pour the liquid into it, stirring thoroughly with a wooden spoon to incorporate all the flour into the liquid and so make a smooth batter.

4 Pour into the prepared loaf tin and bake in the hot oven for 35–40 minutes until risen and golden brown. To check if it is cooked, insert a skewer into the centre of the loaf: if it comes out clean, it is cooked. Transfer to a wire rack and leave to cool completely before serving.

chicken stock

Makes 1.5–1.75 litres/2½–3 pints/6–7 cups.

1 Break up 1 large chicken carcass and place in a large saucepan. Add 1 chopped onion, the chopped white part of 1 leek, 1 chopped celery stick, 1 chopped large carrot, 6 parsley stalks, 1 bay leaf, 1 thyme sprig, 6 peppercorns, ½ tsp sea salt and 2 litres/3 pints/8 cups water.

2 Bring to the boil, then turn the heat down, cover with a lid and leave to simmer for 3 hours. Leave to cool, then strain into a non-metallic container.

3 As soon as the stock is cold, remove and discard the layer of fat that will have separated out and be sitting on the surface. Unless you are using the stock immediately, cover and store in the fridge for 2–3 days, or freeze for later use.

fish stock

Makes about 3 litres/5 pints/12 cups.

1. Wash 2kg/4lb 8oz fish bones (preferably from white fish) thoroughly and break up. Place in a large saucepan with 1 chopped onion, the chopped white part of 1 leek, 1 chopped large carrot, 6 parsley stalks, 6 peppercorns, $^{1}/_{2}$ tsp sea salt and 3 litres/5 pints/12 cups water.
2. Bring to the boil, then turn the heat down, cover with a lid and leave to simmer for 40 minutes. Leave to cool, then strain into a non-metallic container.
3. When the stock is cold, cover and store in the fridge for 1–2 days, or freeze for later use.

vegetable stock

Makes 1–1.25 litres/$1^{3}/_{4}$–2 pints/ 4–5 cups.

1. Place 2 chopped onions, the chopped white part of 2 leeks, 2 chopped celery sticks, 3 chopped large carrots, 1 small handful parsley stalks, 2 bay leaves, 12 peppercorns, $^{1}/_{2}$ tsp sea salt and 1.5 litres/$2^{1}/_{2}$ pints/6 cups water in a large saucepan.
2. Bring to the boil, then turn the heat down, cover with a lid and leave to simmer for 40 minutes. Leave to cool, then strain into a non-metallic container.
3. When the stock is cold, cover and store in the fridge for 3–4 days, or freeze for later use.

breakfasts

Flick through these pages and you'll find a mouth-watering selection of breakfasts to savour, from quick bites on the run to more leisurely meals. Here are juices and smoothies, mueslis, crêpes and muffins, omelettes and full breakfasts. Dive into a Summer Berry Smoothie, which can be made in minutes, or a Blueberry and Banana Muffin, which you can take with you as you head out, for example, or kick back and enjoy Scrambled Eggs with Bacon and freshly baked bread. Start your day with a nutrient-rich meal and you'll feel the difference immediately – your energy levels will soar, you'll feel more alert and focused, and you won't be so tempted to eat forbidden snacks throughout the day.

summer berry smoothie

PREPARATION TIME **5 MINUTES, PLUS 30 MINUTES DEFROSTING TIME** SERVES **2**

500g/1lb 2oz raspberries, strawberries, blueberries and/or red currants, or 1 large bag frozen mixed summer berries

75g/2½oz silken tofu, cut into small chunks

500ml/17fl oz/2 cups soya milk

1–2 tbsp clear honey

1. If using frozen berries, take out of the freezer and leave to stand at room temperature for about 30 minutes, to defrost slightly, before making the smoothie.
2. Put all the berries and/or currants into a liquidizer or food processor. Add the tofu, milk and honey to taste, and blend until smooth and creamy. Serve immediately.

mango, passionfruit and banana smoothie

PREPARATION TIME **5 MINUTES** SERVES **2**

1 large ripe mango

2 passionfruits, cut in half

1 banana, thickly sliced

1. With a sharp knife, carefully slice the mango down the sides, avoiding the stone. Cut the flesh inside the slices into small squares, cutting down to the peel but not piercing it, and scoop out with a spoon. Peel the remains of the mango and slice the flesh from the stone. Place all the mango flesh in a liquidizer or food processor.
2. Scoop out the pulp and seeds from the passionfruits and add to the mango with the banana.
3. Blend until smooth and creamy, then serve immediately.

pineapple, nectarine and ginger juice

PREPARATION TIME **5 MINUTES** SERVES **2**

1 large, ripe pineapple
4 ripe nectarines or peaches, pitted and cut into quarters
3cm/1¼in piece fresh ginger, peeled and coarsely chopped

1 Trim the woody base and green top off the pineapple and, holding it upright, slice off and discard the skin, including the "eyes". Slice the flesh down the length of the fruit all around into long, thin slices, stopping when you reach the core.
2 Press the pineapple and nectarine pieces with the chopped ginger through an electric juicer and serve immediately.

pomegranate, grape and kiwi juice

PREPARATION TIME **10 MINUTES** SERVES **2**

2 pomegranates, cut in half
1 large bunch seedless grapes, about 700g/1lb 9oz total weight, destalked
2 kiwi fruits, cut in half

1 Hold each pomegranate half above a large mixing bowl and bash the outer skin with the back of a wooden spoon, so that the fleshy red seeds fall into the bowl. You'll need to bash the skin a few times before the pips begin to fall out, but they will.
2 Set 2 tbsp of the seeds on one side and press the remainder with the grapes and kiwi fruits through an electric juicer. Pour into glasses, add the reserved seeds and serve.

muesli with almond milk

PREPARATION TIME **10 MINUTES, PLUS OVERNIGHT SOAKING TIME** SERVES **4**

150g/5oz/1½ cups jumbo oats
50g/2oz/heaped ⅓ cup barley flakes
50g/2oz/heaped ⅓ cup hazelnuts, coarsely chopped
50g/2oz/⅓ cup almonds, coarsely chopped
50g/2oz sugar-free dried mango, coarsely chopped
50g/2oz sugar-free dried cranberries
50g/2oz sugar-free dried figs, coarsely chopped
3 tbsp linseed

Almond milk:
225g/8oz/1½ cups whole blanched almonds
1–2 tbsp clear honey

1 To make the almond milk, place the blanched almonds in a bowl, cover with 750ml/1¼ pints/3 cups water and leave to soak overnight or for at least 12 hours.
2 The next day, put the almonds in a liquidizer, add 125ml/4fl oz/½ cup of the soaking liquid and blend. With the motor running, pour the remaining liquid in gradually and the honey to taste, blending thoroughly to a fine milk. (This will make about 1 litre/1¾ pints/4 cups.) You can store the almond milk in an airtight container in the fridge for up to 3 days.
3 In a large mixing bowl, combine all the dry ingredients, then spoon into bowls. Serve with the almond milk, or use soya milk if you prefer.

To make a gluten-free version of this muesli, you can use 100g/3½oz/⅔ cup rice flakes and 100g/3½oz/⅔ cup buckwheat flakes instead of the oats and barley flakes. Alternatively, you could try 200g/7oz/2 cups quinoa flakes.

bircher muesli

PREPARATION TIME **5 MINUTES, PLUS OVERNIGHT SOAKING TIME** SERVES **4**

200g/7oz/2 cups rolled oats
350ml/12floz/scant 1½ cups apple juice
2 apples
50g/2oz sugar-free dried apple, chopped
125g/4oz soya yogurt
100g/3½oz seasonal berries, such as raspberries and blueberries

1 Put the oats in a large mixing bowl and pour over the apple juice to cover them. Cover the bowl and leave to soak overnight in the fridge.
2 In the morning, peel and grate the apples and add to the oat mixture. Stir in the dried apple and yogurt.
3 Spoon the mixture into bowls. Scatter the berries over each helping and serve.

VARIATION

To make a gluten-free version of bircher muesli, you can use 200g/7oz/1⅓ cups buckwheat flakes instead of the oats. Alternatively, you could try 200g/7oz/2 cups quinoa flakes, but you will need an extra 150ml/5fl oz/scant ⅔ cup apple juice.

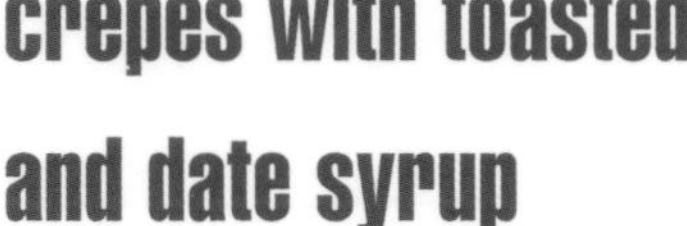

crêpes with toasted coconut flakes and date syrup

PREPARATION TIME **5 MINUTES, PLUS 30 MINUTES STANDING TIME**
COOKING TIME **15–20 MINUTES** SERVES **4**

50g/2oz/scant 1/3 cup rice flour
50g/2oz/scant 1/2 cup gram flour
1 pinch salt
1 egg, beaten
250ml/9fl oz/1 cup soya milk
75g/2 1/2oz/1 cup unsweetened coconut flakes
15g/ 1/2oz dairy-free margarine
3 tbsp date syrup

1 Sift the flours with the salt into a large mixing bowl. Make a well in the centre and add the egg, beating slowly with a wooden spoon to incorporate the flours. Slowly beat in the milk, gradually drawing in the flours to form a smooth batter. Cover and leave to stand for at least 10 minutes or up to 30 minutes in the fridge.

2 Meanwhile, heat a 20cm/8in heavy-based frying pan over a medium heat until hot. Toss in the coconut flakes and dry-fry until lightly browned, turning frequently to prevent burning. Tip the coconut into a bowl. Wipe the frying pan clean and return to the heat. Add the margarine and heat until melted, making sure it covers the base of the pan.

3 Pour 125ml/4fl oz/ 1/2 cup prepared batter into the pan and tilt the pan so that the base is completely covered with the mixture. (It needs to be thicker than for a normal crêpe because of the lack of gluten to hold it together.) Cook for 2–3 minutes, until the base of the crêpe is golden. Using a wooden spatula, carefully loosen the crêpe from the base, then flip it over onto the other side (or toss it if you are feeling confident). Cook for a further 1–2 minutes.

4 Repeat with the remaining batter, stacking the freshly cooked crêpes between sheets of non-stick baking parchment to prevent them sticking together and keep them warm. Note that the later crêpes will take only 1–2 minutes on each side as the pan will have heated up.

5 When all four crêpes are cooked, fold them into quarters, drizzle a little date syrup over the top, sprinkle with the toasted coconut flakes and serve.

blueberry and banana muffins

PREPARATION TIME **10 MINUTES** COOKING TIME **20–25 MINUTES** MAKES **10**

75g/2½oz dairy-free margarine, softened, plus extra for greasing
50g/2oz/¼ cup fruit sugar
1 large egg, lightly beaten
100ml/3½fl oz/scant ½ cup soya milk
100g/3½oz/heaped ⅔ cup rice flour
100g/3½oz/scant 1 cup gram flour
1 tsp gluten-free baking powder
2 small bananas, mashed
150g/5oz blueberries

1 Preheat the oven to 200°C/400°F/Gas 6. Grease 10 paper muffin cases and place them in a muffin tray. Put the margarine and sugar in a large mixing bowl and, using a hand-held electric whisk, beat well until light and fluffy. Gradually beat in the egg, a little at a time, then beat in the soya milk.

2 Sift in the flours and baking powder and stir quickly with a wooden spoon until mixed. Be careful not to overmix, and don't worry if you can still see lumps in the mixture.

3 Carefully fold in the mashed bananas and the blueberries, then spoon the mixture into the prepared paper cases, filling each one about two-thirds full.

4 Bake in the hot oven for 20–25 minutes until well risen and just firm to the touch, or until a skewer inserted into the centre comes out clean. Take the muffins out of the oven and either eat them warm or transfer them in their paper cases to a wire rack to cool.

herb omelette with creamy mushrooms

PREPARATION TIME **5 MINUTES** COOKING TIME **10 MINUTES** SERVES **2**

4 eggs

35g/1½oz dairy-free margarine

2 heaped tbsp chopped mint leaves

2 heaped tbsp chopped basil leaves

2 tbsp olive oil

150g/5oz closed-cup mushrooms, cut into quarters

200g/7oz soya yogurt

sea salt and freshly ground black pepper

1 Beat the eggs in a bowl, then season lightly with salt and pepper. Heat the margarine in a 20cm/8in heavy-based frying pan, making sure the base is well covered in the hot fat. Pour the egg mixture into the pan and sprinkle over half the chopped mint and basil. As the egg begins to set, keep lifting the edges gently and tilting the pan to let the uncooked egg trickle underneath. After 5–6 minutes the base of the omelette will be golden and the top almost set, but still soft.

2 Meanwhile, heat the oil in a large, heavy-based saucepan. Add the mushrooms and cook over a medium heat for 3–4 minutes, stirring frequently. Using a whisk or hand-held electric blender, blend the yogurt. Turn the heat down to low, pour the yogurt into the pan, add the remaining herbs and season lightly with salt and pepper. Gently cook the mixture for 2–3 minutes, making sure not to cook it for too long as the yogurt may curdle.

3 When the omelette is just set, tilt the pan away from you and, using a metal spatula, carefully fold it in half. Leave it to stand for 30 seconds, then cut into two portions. Serve immediately with the creamy mushrooms.

scrambled eggs with bacon

PREPARATION TIME **5 MINUTES** COOKING TIME **6 MINUTES** SERVES **4**

8 rashers nitrate-free bacon, rinds removed
8 eggs
6 tbsp sugar-free soya milk
50g/2oz dairy-free margarine
sea salt and freshly ground black pepper

1 Preheat the grill to high. Place the bacon rashers on the grill rack and cook under the hot grill for 2–3 minutes on each side, or until cooked to your liking.
2 While the bacon is cooking, beat the eggs in a small mixing bowl. Stir in the soya milk and season lightly with salt and pepper. Melt the margarine in a heavy-based saucepan over a very low heat. Pour in the egg mixture and cook very gently, stirring frequently, for 4–5 minutes until the mixture thickens but is still slightly runny.
3 Serve immediately with the bacon and slices of toast of your choice (see bread recipes on pages 23–4).

baked beans with hash browns

PREPARATION TIME **20 MINUTES, PLUS OVERNIGHT SOAKING TIME** COOKING TIME **1½–2 HOURS** SERVES **2**

125g/4oz/scant $^{2}/_{3}$ cup dried haricot beans, or 410g/14oz tin salt-free haricot beans in water, drained and rinsed
4 large, vine-ripened tomatoes
1 tbsp olive oil
1 onion, chopped
6 tbsp tomato purée
1 tbsp chopped thyme leaves
sea salt

Hash browns:
4 potatoes, peeled and grated
1 small onion, grated
1 egg, beaten
1 tbsp rice flour
1 tsp sea salt
1 tbsp olive oil

1 If using dried haricot beans, place in a bowl, cover with cold water and leave to soak overnight or for at least 12 hours.

2 The next day, drain the beans and rinse thoroughly. Put in a large saucepan, cover with fresh water and bring to the boil. Boil rapidly for 10 minutes, then turn the heat down, cover with a lid and leave to simmer for 1–1$^{1}/_{2}$ hours until tender. Drain thoroughly.

3 Meanwhile, cut a cross in the skin of each tomato with a sharp knife, place in a heatproof bowl and cover with boiling water. Leave to stand for 2 minutes, then remove the tomatoes, peel off and discard the skins and coarsely chop the flesh.

4 Heat the oil in a heavy-based saucepan over a medium heat. Add the onion and cook for 2–3 minutes until golden. Add the remaining ingredients, including the beans, and 125ml/4fl oz/$^{1}/_{2}$ cup water, bring to the boil, stir well, then turn the heat down, cover with a lid and leave to simmer for 30 minutes. Season to taste.

5 Meanwhile, make the hash browns. Mix the potatoes and onion in a bowl. Tip the mixture onto a clean tea towel, wrap it around the mixture and squeeze well so that it soaks up the excess moisture. Return to the bowl, stir in the egg, flour and salt and mix well.

6 Divide the mixture into six and shape each portion into a small, round cake. Heat the oil in a heavy-based frying pan over a medium heat. Place three of the hash brown rounds in the pan, flatten them slightly with the back of a wooden spoon and cook for 5–6 minutes on each side until crisp and golden brown. Remove from the pan with a slotted spatula and keep warm. Repeat with the remaining hash browns. Serve with the baked beans.

lunches

Wherever you are and whatever you're doing, you'll find exactly the recipe you need in the following pages. Whether you want to pack something into a lunchbox or take a bite for a picnic, you'll discover pâtés, potato cakes and tabbouleh. If you feel like having soup – either a hearty, warming one such as Pea and Ham Soup or a light Chilled Avocado Soup for a summer's day – you'll find a delicious selection here. There are salads, from Thai-style Chicken Salad with Rice Vermicelli to Oven-roasted Butternut Squash and Beetroot Salad, and delicious, comforting favourites, such as Parma Ham and Rocket Pizza, as well as more exotic dishes, such as Prawn and Vegetable Tempura. Many of these recipes can be prepared in advance and stored, or they can be made quickly in the morning before you leave for the day.

smoked salmon pâté

PREPARATION TIME **3–5 MINUTES** SERVES **2**

250g/9oz smoked salmon
125g/4oz silken tofu
1 tbsp sugar-free soya milk
juice of 1/2 lemon
1 handful dill, finely chopped, plus extra to serve
freshly ground black pepper

1 Place all the ingredients in a bowl and blend briefly using a hand-held electric blender to form a coarse paste. Alternatively, blend all the ingredients in a liquidizer or food processor.
2 Serve spread thickly on slices of bread (see pages 23–4) and topped with dill or put in a container for a lunchbox.

VARIATION

For an Asian-style pâté, replace the milk, lemon, dill and pepper with ½–1 large red chilli, deseeded and finely chopped, 1cm/½in piece fresh ginger, peeled and finely chopped, 1 large garlic clove, crushed, and the juice of 1 lime.

potato cakes with smoked salmon

PREPARATION TIME **10 MINUTES** COOKING TIME **30–40 MINUTES** SERVES **2**

250g/9oz potatoes, peeled and cut into chunks
50g/2oz dairy-free margarine
3 tbsp rice flour, plus extra for dusting
30g/1¼oz/¼ cup gram flour
½ tsp sea salt
1 tsp gluten-free baking powder
1 large egg, beaten
2 tbsp olive oil
250g/9oz smoked salmon

1 Put the potatoes in a saucepan and cover with cold water. Place over a high heat and bring to the boil, then turn the heat down, cover with a lid and leave to simmer for 15–20 minutes until tender. Drain and mash well with the margarine until smooth.
2 Sift the flours into a large mixing bowl. Stir in the salt and baking powder and make a well in the centre of the mixture. Pour the beaten egg into the well, then add the mashed potato and, using a wooden spoon, gradually draw the flour mixture into the egg and potato, mixing until all the ingredients are thoroughly combined.
3 Turn the mixture out onto a surface that has been liberally dusted with rice flour. Divide into six pieces. With cold hands, shape each piece into a ball, then flatten to form a small, round cake and dust lightly with more rice flour. You'll find the mixture sticky, so try to work quickly before your hands warm up and keep sprinkling more rice flour onto the work surface whenever you need to.
4 Heat half of the oil in a large, heavy-based frying pan. Add three potato cakes and cook for 4–5 minutes on each side until golden brown. Remove from the pan, drain on kitchen paper, then repeat with the second batch.
5 Top each potato cake with a slice of smoked salmon and serve. Alternatively, leave to cool and put in a container for a lunchbox.

artichoke pâté

PREPARATION TIME **15 MINUTES** COOKING TIME **1–40 MINUTES** SERVES **4**

8 artichokes, stems and very outer leaves removed, or 400g/14oz bottled or tinned artichoke hearts in water or oil, drained (1 tbsp oil reserved)
1 tbsp olive oil (optional)
2 garlic cloves, chopped
25g/1oz rocket, coarsely chopped (optional)
sea salt

1 If using fresh artichokes, place in two large saucepans of boiling water and return to the boil, then turn the heat down, cover with a lid and leave to simmer for 30–40 minutes until you can pull the leaves off the artichokes easily. Drain, leave until cool enough to handle, and remove all the leaves, then scrape out the hairy "chokes" of the vegetables, leaving the bases, known as the "hearts".
2 If using artichokes preserved in oil, use 1 tbsp oil from the bottle or tin; if not, use olive oil. Heat the oil in a small, heavy-based saucepan. Add the garlic and cook for 30 seconds until just starting to brown. Tip into a bowl, add the artichoke hearts and rocket, if using, and blend with a hand-held electric blender to form a smooth, creamy paste. Season lightly with salt. Alternatively, blend in a liquidizer or food processor.
3 Spread onto slices of bread (see pages 23–4) or put in a container for a lunchbox.

quinoa tabbouleh

PREPARATION TIME **10 MINUTES** COOKING TIME **15–20 MINUTES** SERVES **4**

150g/5oz/¾ cup quinoa
4 vine-ripened tomatoes
2 bunches flat-leaf parsley, finely chopped
2 bunches mint, finely chopped
6 spring onions, finely sliced

Dressing:
6 tbsp extra virgin olive oil
juice of 2 lemons
sea salt and freshly ground black pepper

1 Place the quinoa in a sieve and rinse well under cold running water. Tranfer to a saucepan and pour over 250ml/9fl oz/1 cup cold water. Bring to the boil, then turn the heat down, cover with a lid and leave to simmer for 15–20 minutes until the quinoa is tender and the water has been absorbed. Transfer to a serving bowl and leave to cool. (If any water is left in the pan, drain the quinoa thoroughly through a sieve first.)
2 Meanwhile, with a sharp knife, make a cross in the skin of each tomato, then place in a large, heatproof bowl and cover with boiling water. Leave to stand for 2–3 minutes. Drain, then peel off and discard the skins. Halve each tomato, scoop out and discard the seeds, dice the flesh and add to the quinoa in the bowl. Stir in the parsley, mint and spring onions.
3 Whisk together the dressing ingredients in a jug or bowl and season lightly, then pour over the top of the tabbouleh, stirring thoroughly so that the ingredients are well combined. Serve or put in a container for a lunchbox.

pea and ham soup

PREPARATION TIME **10 MINUTES** COOKING TIME **20 MINUTES**
ADDITIONAL TIME **MAKING THE STOCK** SERVES **4**

2 tbsp olive oil
1 onion, finely chopped
2 large garlic cloves, crushed
1 carrot, peeled and chopped
½ large or 1 small leek, chopped
750g/1lb 9oz/5 cups fresh or frozen peas
1 bay leaf
1.2 litres/2 pints/scant 5 cups Chicken or Vegetable Stock (see pages 24–5), or vegetable stock made from gluten-, yeast- and dairy-free stock powder
250g/9oz nitrate-free air-dried ham, such as Serrano, chopped
sea salt and freshly ground black pepper

1. Heat the oil in a large, heavy-based saucepan over a low heat. Add the onion and cook for 2–3 minutes until just starting to turn golden brown. Stir in the garlic, then add the carrot and leek and cook for 1 minute.
2. Add the peas and the bay leaf and cook for 5 minutes, then pour in the stock. Turn up the heat slightly and bring to a gentle boil, then turn the heat down, cover with a lid and leave to simmer for 5 minutes. Stir in half the ham, using all the pieces with any fat on them, and cook for 5 minutes.
3. Remove the bay leaf and blend the mixture briefly in the pan using a hand-held electric blender to make a coarsely textured soup. Alternatively, blend the soup in a liquidizer or food processor, return to the pan and heat through. Stir in the remaining ham, season lightly with salt and pepper and serve with slices of bread (see pages 23–4).

tom yum soup

PREPARATION TIME **10 MINUTES** COOKING TIME **25 MINUTES**
ADDITIONAL TIME **MAKING THE STOCK** SERVES **4**

1cm/½in piece fresh ginger, peeled and chopped
1 heaped tbsp chopped coriander leaves and stems, plus whole leaves to serve
1 shallot, chopped
2 large red chillies, deseeded and chopped
1 tbsp olive oil
6 lemongrass stalks, white ends sliced
2 tbsp Thai fish sauce
2 litres/3½ pints/8 cups Vegetable Stock (see page 25), or stock made from gluten-, yeast- and dairy-free stock powder
100g/3½oz closed-cup mushrooms, sliced
250g/9oz cooked, peeled prawns
juice of 1 lime

1 Put the ginger, chopped coriander, shallot, chillies and oil in a food processor and blend to form a coarse paste. Tip into a large, heavy-based saucepan and add the lemongrass, fish sauce and stock. Bring to the boil over a medium heat, then turn the heat down, cover with a lid and leave to simmer for 15 minutes.

2 Strain through a fine sieve and return to the cleaned pan. Add the mushrooms, return to the boil, then turn the heat down, cover with a lid and leave to simmer for 5 minutes. Add the prawns and cook for 1–2 minutes, then stir in the lime juice. Check the seasoning, adding more fish sauce if required. Sprinkle with coriander leaves and serve with slices of bread (see pages 23–4).

crab bisque

PREPARATION TIME **10 MINUTES** COOKING TIME **35 MINUTES**
ADDITIONAL TIME **MAKING THE STOCK** SERVES **4**

50g/2oz dairy-free margarine
½ onion, chopped
1 celery stick, chopped
1 carrot, peeled and chopped
1 bay leaf
1.25 litres/generous 2 pints/5 cups Fish Stock (see page 25), or vegetable stock made from gluten-, yeast- and dairy-free stock powder
100ml/3½fl oz/scant ½ cup organic dry white wine
2 vine-ripened tomatoes, coarsely chopped
1 tbsp tomato purée
¼ tsp cayenne pepper
450g/1lb cooked crabmeat, about half brown and half white meat
150g/5oz soya yogurt
sea salt and freshly ground black pepper

1 Melt the margarine in a large, heavy-based saucepan. Add the onion, celery, carrot and bay leaf and cook over a gentle heat for 2–3 minutes. Stir in the stock, wine, chopped tomatoes and tomato purée, increase the heat and bring to the boil. Turn the heat down, cover with a lid and leave to simmer for 20 minutes. Remove the bay leaf.
2 Blend in the pan using a hand-held electric blender. Alternatively, blend in a liquidizer or food processor, return to the pan and heat through. Stir in the cayenne and crabmeat, bring to the boil, then turn the heat down, cover with a lid and leave to simmer for 10 minutes. Season lightly with salt and pepper.
3 Using a whisk or a hand-held electric blender, blend the yogurt until smooth, then add to the soup and stir in thoroughly. Serve with slices of bread (see pages 23–4).

courgette and spicy seeds soup

PREPARATION TIME **10 MINUTES** COOKING TIME **25–35 MINUTES**
ADDITIONAL TIME **MAKING THE STOCK** SERVES **4**

1½ tbsp olive oil
1 onion, chopped
2 garlic cloves, crushed
4 large courgettes, about 750g/1lb 9oz total weight, thickly sliced
250g/9oz potatoes, peeled and thickly sliced
500ml/17fl oz/2 cups Vegetable Stock (see page 25), or stock made from gluten-, yeast- and dairy-free stock powder
½–1 tsp chilli flakes
sea salt and freshly ground black pepper

Spicy seeds:
100g/3½oz/¾ cup sunflower seeds
100g/3½oz/¾ cup sesame seeds
50g/2oz/⅓ cup pumpkin seeds
4 tbsp tamari soy sauce

1 Preheat the oven to 150°C/300°F/Gas 2. Heat the oil in a large, heavy-based saucepan over a low heat. Add the onion and cook for 2–3 minutes until golden. Stir in the garlic, then add the courgettes and potatoes and cook for 3–4 minutes, stirring occasionally. Pour in the stock and bring to the boil, then turn the heat down, cover with a lid and leave to simmer for 20–25 minutes until the potatoes are soft.

2 Meanwhile, prepare the spicy seeds. Spread the seeds over a baking tray and sprinkle with the tamari soy sauce. Cook in the hot oven for 15 minutes. Take the seeds out of the oven, turn them over and return to the oven for a further 10–15 minutes until golden brown.

3 Stir the spicy seeds into the soup with the chilli flakes to taste. Blend briefly in the pan using a hand-held electric blender to make a coarsely textured soup or for longer for a smoother result. Alternatively, blend in a liquidizer or food processor and return to the pan and heat through. Season lightly with salt and pepper and serve with slices of bread (see pages 23–4).

VARIATION

For a lighter version of this soup, omit the potatoes and use only 250ml/9fl oz/1 cup stock and ¼–½ tsp chilli flakes.

chilled avocado soup

PREPARATION TIME **10 MINUTES, PLUS 2 HOURS CHILLING TIME**
ADDITIONAL TIME **MAKING THE STOCK** SERVES **4**

5 ripe avocados, peeled, pitted and chopped
1 shallot, finely chopped
1 large garlic clove, finely chopped
juice of 1 lemon
1 tbsp olive oil
150g/5oz soya yogurt
400ml/14fl oz/1¾ cups cold Chicken or Vegetable Stock (see pages 24–5), or cold vegetable stock made from gluten-, yeast- and dairy-free stock powder
2 heaped tbsp chopped mint leaves
sea salt and freshly ground black papper

1 Put the avocados, shallot, garlic, lemon juice, oil and yogurt in a food processor and blend until smooth. With the motor running, gradually pour in the stock. Add half of the chopped mint and blend briefly to mix in. Season lightly with salt and pepper.
2 Pour the soup into a large bowl, cover with cling film and leave in the fridge for 2 hours.
3 Stir in the remaining mint and serve with slices of bread (see pages 23–4).

roast tomato and sage soup

PREPARATION TIME **10 MINUTES** COOKING TIME **1½ HOURS**
ADDITIONAL TIME **MAKING THE STOCK** SERVES **4**

16 large vine-ripened tomatoes, about 1.8kg/4lb total weight, cut in half
4 large garlic cloves, unpeeled
3 tbsp olive oil
1 red onion, chopped
1½ tbsp chopped sage leaves
125ml/4fl oz/½ cup Vegetable Stock (see page 25), or stock made from gluten-, yeast- and dairy-free stock powder
sea salt and freshly ground black pepper

1 Preheat the oven to 180°C/350°F/Gas 4. Arrange the tomato halves cut-side up on a baking tray with the garlic cloves. Roast in the hot oven for 1¼ hours until browned and soft. Remove from the oven and leave to cool slightly.
2 Heat the oil in a large, heavy-based saucepan over a low heat. Add the onion and cook for 2–3 minutes until it starts to turn golden.
3 With a metal spoon, scrape the flesh away from the tomato skins and add to the saucepan, discarding the skins. Squeeze the flesh out of the garlic cloves and add to the pan, discarding the skins. Stir the chopped sage into the mixture and bring to the boil, then turn the heat down, cover with a lid and leave to simmer for 10 minutes, stirring occasionally.
4 Blend in the pan using a hand-held electric blender until smooth, adding the vegetable stock gradually until the soup is thick but still runny. Alternatively, blend in a liquidizer or food processor, then return to the pan and heat through. Season lightly with salt and pepper, and serve hot or chilled with slices of bread (see pages 23–4).

thai-style chicken salad with rice vermicelli

PREPARATION TIME **10 MINUTES** COOKING TIME **30–35 MINUTES** SERVES **4**

2 skinless, boneless chicken breasts
2 tbsp olive oil
150g/5½oz rice vermicelli
4 spring onions, finely sliced
1 garlic clove, finely chopped
2cm/¾in piece fresh ginger, peeled and finely chopped
½ large red chilli, deseeded and finely chopped
1 handful chopped mint leaves
2 handfuls chopped coriander leaves
1 handful chopped basil leaves
½ cucumber, cut into matchsticks
2 carrots, peeled and cut into matchsticks
1 courgette, cut into matchsticks
juice of 1 lime
1 tsp Thai fish sauce
2 handfuls unsalted peanuts, chopped, to serve

1. Preheat the oven to 180°C/350°F/Gas 4. Put the chicken breasts in an ovenproof dish, drizzle over 1 tbsp of the oil and cover. Cook in the hot oven for 20–25 minutes until cooked through. To test that the chicken is cooked, prick with the tip of a sharp knife and check that the juice that runs out of it is clear, not pink. Take the chicken out of the oven and leave to cool.
2. Put the vermicelli in a large heatproof bowl, cover with boiling water and leave to stand for 5 minutes until soft. Tip into a colander and rinse well under cold running water.
3. Heat a large wok or frying pan over a high heat until hot. Add the remaining oil and swirl it around the wok. Toss in the spring onions and stir-fry for about 1 minute until they start to turn golden. Add the garlic, ginger and chilli and cook for 1 minute, then tip into a large salad bowl. Add the chopped herbs and the vegetable matchsticks.
4. Shred the cooled chicken and add to the bowl, along with the lime juice and fish sauce. Add the noodles and stir thoroughly until all the ingredients are well combined. Sprinkle with the peanuts and serve.

beef carpaccio

PREPARATION TIME **5 MINUTES** SERVES **4**

450g/1lb beef fillet steak, very thinly sliced into about 12 slices
50g/2oz baby leaf spinach
50g/2oz rocket
1 large handful flat-leaf parsley, coarsely chopped
12 cherry tomatoes, cut in half horizontally

Dressing:
1 garlic clove, crushed
juice of ½ lemon
4 tbsp extra virgin olive oil
sea salt and freshly ground black pepper

1 Arrange the steak slices on a large piece of cling film, making sure they are all separated, and cover with another piece of film. Using a rolling pin, roll the slices of meat out until they become paper-thin.
2 Whisk together the dressing ingredients in a jug or bowl, seasoning lightly.
3 Serve the steak slices with the spinach, rocket and parsley and the tomato halves, all drizzled with the dressing.

borlotti bean and tuna salad

PREPARATION TIME **10 MINUTES, PLUS OVERNIGHT SOAKING TIME**
COOKING TIME **2½ HOURS** SERVES **4**

100g/3½oz/½ cup dried borlotti beans, or 410g/14oz tin salt-free borlotti beans in water, drained and rinsed
400g/14oz vine-ripened tomatoes, cut into quarters
2 tbsp olive oil
100g/3½oz green beans, cut in half
4 tuna steaks
1 handful baby spinach leaves
1 handful rocket

Dressing:
3 tbsp extra virgin olive oil
1½ tbsp balsamic vinegar
sea salt and freshly ground black pepper

1 If using dried borlotti beans, place them in a bowl, cover with cold water and leave to soak overnight or for at least 12 hours.
2 The next day, preheat the oven to 140°C/275°F/Gas 1. Arrange the tomatoes in a single layer on a baking tray and drizzle with 1½ tbsp of the olive oil. Roast in the oven for 2½ hours until dried.
3 Meanwhile, drain the beans and rinse thoroughly. Put in a large saucepan, cover with fresh water and bring to the boil. Boil rapidly for 10 minutes, then turn the heat down, cover with a lid and leave to simmer for 1–1½ hours until tender. Drain thoroughly.
4 Place the green beans in a steamer and steam for 1–2 minutes until just tender.
5 Preheat the grill to high. Brush the tuna lightly on both sides with the remaining olive oil, then place on the grill rack and cook under the hot grill for 2–3 minutes on each side. Alternatively, fry in the remaining oil over a medium-high heat for 2–3 minutes on each side.
6 While the tuna is cooking, put the spinach and rocket in a large bowl and mix in the cooked or tinned borlotti beans and the green beans. Take the tomatoes out of the oven and add them with their oil. Whisk the dressing ingredients together in a jug or bowl, seasoning lightly, and pour over the salad, mixing until well combined. Serve the tuna with the salad.

stir-fried squid salad

PREPARATION TIME **10 MINUTES** COOKING TIME **2–3 MINUTES** SERVES **4**

1kg/2lb 4oz baby squid

2 tbsp olive oil

1 large red chilli, deseeded and finely chopped

1 bunch spring onions, finely chopped

1 tbsp Thai fish sauce

3 tbsp chopped coriander leaves

3 heaped tbsp chopped mint leaves

Salad:

4 Little Gem lettuces, leaves torn in half

65g/2½oz rocket

1 cucumber, cut into thin strips

1 red pepper, deseeded and cut into thin strips

Dressing:

6 tbsp extra virgin olive oil

2 tbsp lemon juice

1 tbsp chopped mint leaves

1 tbsp chopped coriander leaves

1 To prepare the squid, pull the tentacles out of the sacs and cut them away from the beak part of the head that holds them together. Feel inside each sac for the transparent quill, or backbone, and remove any that you find, then pull off the outer membrane, if present. Finally, rinse the sacs and tentacles under cold running water and pat dry on kitchen paper. Using a sharp knife, cut down one side of the squid sacs and open out flat. Score the insides with a diamond pattern, then cut into wide strips about 5cm/2in long. Leave the tentacles intact.

2 Place the salad ingredients in a large salad bowl and mix together well.

3 Whisk together all the dressing ingredients in a jug or bowl.

4 Heat the oil in a wok or large frying pan over a high heat. Add the squid, chilli, spring onions and fish sauce and cook, stirring continuously, for 2–3 minutes until the squid has turned a light golden colour. Take the wok off the heat and stir in the chopped herbs.

5 Spoon over the prepared salad and cover with the dressing. Serve either warm or cold.

broad bean, pea, smoked tofu and mint salad

PREPARATION TIME **20 MINUTES** COOKING TIME **3–4 MINUTES** SERVES **4**

1kg/2lb 4oz broad beans in their pods, shelled (450g/1lb/2½ cups shelled)
1kg/2lb 4oz peas in their pods, shelled (450g/1lb/3 cups shelled)
5 mint sprigs
150g/5oz smoked tofu

Dressing:
3 tbsp extra virgin olive oil
juice of 1 lime
1 heaped tbsp chopped mint leaves
sea salt and freshly ground black pepper

1 Place the beans and peas in a steamer. Add the mint sprigs, place over a high heat and cook for 3–4 minutes until just tender. Remove and discard the mint.
2 Rinse the vegetables under cold running water, then drain well and tip into a large salad bowl. Crumble the tofu over the top.
3 Whisk together the dressing ingredients in a jug or bowl and season lightly with salt and pepper. Pour over the salad and serve.

oven-roasted butternut squash and beetroot salad

PREPARATION TIME **15 MINUTES** COOKING TIME **40–45 MINUTES** SERVES **4**

800g/2lb 8oz butternut or other squash, peeled, deseeded and cut into chunks
3 tbsp olive oil
600g/1lb 8oz fresh beetroots, washed, peeled, trimmed and cut into quarters
150g/6oz/1 cup pine nuts
1 large avocado
½ tbsp lemon juice (optional)
150g/5oz mixed salad leaves, such as lettuce, baby leaf spinach and red chard
50g/2oz rocket

Dressing:
6 tbsp extra virgin olive oil
2 tbsp balsamic vinegar

1. Preheat the oven to 180°C/350°F/Gas 4. Arrange the pieces of squash on a baking tray and drizzle over half of the olive oil. Repeat with the beetroot quarters on another tray. Roast the vegetables in the hot oven for 40–45 minutes until cooked through.
2. Meanwhile, heat a heavy-based frying pan over a medium heat. Add the pine nuts and dry-fry until just starting to turn golden. Remove from the heat.
3. Peel the avocado, remove the stone and slice the flesh. (If you want to prepare the salad ahead of time, dip the avocado slices into the lemon juice to avoid it turning brown.) Pile the salad leaves and rocket into a large salad bowl and mix well. Remove the vegetables from the oven and add to the salad, then top with the avocado slices and pine nuts.
4. Whisk the dressing ingredients together in a jug or bowl, pour over the salad and serve.

sweetcorn fritters with salsa salad

PREPARATION TIME **10 MINUTES** COOKING TIME **25–30 MINUTES** MAKES **10**

1 egg white
200g/7oz/1 1/3 cups frozen sweetcorn, defrosted and drained
1/2 red chilli, deseeded and finely chopped
150ml/5fl oz/scant 2/3 cup sugar-free soya milk
1 egg, beaten
1/2 tsp sea salt
55g/2oz/1/2 cup gram flour
1 tsp gluten-free baking powder
olive oil, for frying
mixed salad leaves

Avocado salsa:
1 onion, finely chopped
3 large plum tomatoes, diced
2 avocados, peeled, pitted and diced
juice of 1 lime
handful chopped coriander leaves

1 Whisk the egg white in a small bowl, preferably using a hand-held electric whisk, until it forms soft peaks. Tip the sweetcorn into a large mixing bowl and carefully fold in the whisked egg white, then gently mix in the chilli, soya milk, beaten egg and salt. Sift in the flour and the baking powder and mix thoroughly to form a thick batter.
2 Lightly brush the base of a large, heavy-based frying pan with a little olive oil and place over a low heat. Spoon 2 tbsp of the corn batter into the hot pan to make each fritter (you should be able to fit three or four in the pan). Fry gently for 4–5 minutes on each side until golden brown. Remove from the pan, drain on kitchen paper, keep warm and repeat.
3 Meanwhile, mix all the salsa ingredients together in a bowl.
4 Serve the fritters with the salad leaves and salsa.

smoked salmon, prawn and vegetable sushi

PREPARATION TIME **20–25 MINUTES, PLUS 45–50 MINUTES DRAINING AND COOLING TIME**
COOKING TIME **15–20 MINUTES** SERVES **4**

450g/1lb/heaped 2 cups sushi rice
4 tbsp rice vinegar
25g/1oz fruit sugar
1 tsp sea salt
8 sheets toasted nori seaweed, each about 20 x 18cm/8 x 7¼in
24–32 cooked, peeled, large king prawns, deveined
250g/9oz smoked salmon, cut into strips
2 ripe avocados, peeled, pitted and thickly sliced lengthways
½ cucumber, cut lengthways into thin strips 1cm/½in wide, seeds discarded
¼ tsp wasabi paste, or to taste
tamari soy sauce, for dipping

1 Put the rice in a large mixing bowl and cover with cold water. Swirl the rice around, then drain through a sieve. Repeat until the water stays clear, then leave to drain for 30 minutes.

2 Transfer the rice to a large saucepan and pour 400ml/14fl oz/1¾ cups water over it. Bring to the boil over a medium heat, then turn the heat down, cover with a lid, clear if possible, and leave to simmer for 8–10 minutes until all the water has been absorbed. With the lid still on, remove from the heat and leave to stand for 10–15 minutes.

3 Meanwhile, heat the rice vinegar, sugar and salt in a small saucepan over a low heat until all the sugar has dissolved. Remove from the heat and leave to cool slightly.

4 Spoon the cooked rice into a large, shallow dish. Pour the vinegar mixture over it and, with a wooden spatula, gently fold the liquid into the rice. Leave to cool completely.

5 Lay a sheet of nori, shiny side down, on a clean cloth. Spread 4 heaped tbsp of the cold rice over about a third of the nori up to the edges. Spread a very thin line of wasabi paste on top. Place 3–4 prawns, 4–5 strips of salmon (about 30g/1oz), 3 slices of avocado and then 4–6 strips of cucumber on the rice in a horizontal line, slightly off-centre, nearer the middle of the sheet. Holding the edge of the cloth and the edge of nori nearest to you together, carefully roll the nori over the filling, rolling the cloth with it in order to secure it. Compress the roll slightly so that it holds firmly together. Repeat with the remaining sheets of nori and filling ingredients.

6 Cut each roll into five lengths and serve with a small dish of tamari soy sauce for dipping.

parma ham and rocket pizza

PREPARATION TIME **1 HOUR 25 MINUTES** COOKING TIME **12–15 MINUTES** SERVES **2**

85g/3oz/½ cup rice flour, plus extra for dusting
85g/3oz/¾ cup gram flour
30g/1¼oz/scant ¼ cup maize flour
½ tsp salt
1 tsp easy-blend dried yeast
2 tbsp olive oil
dairy-free margarine, for greasing

Topping:
4 tbsp passata
1½ tbsp tomato purée
150g/5oz nitrate-free Parma ham, thinly sliced
60–100g/2¼–3½oz dairy-free cheese, shaved
1 handful rocket

1 Sift the flours and salt into a large mixing bowl. Add the yeast and mix in well. Make a well in the middle and pour in the oil. Gradually work the flour into the oil, using a wooden spoon or your fingertips, until well blended. Pour in 100ml/3½fl oz/scant ½ cup warm water, a little at a time, and continue mixing to form a soft dough.

2 Turn the dough out onto a surface liberally dusted with rice flour and knead thoroughly for about 10 minutes. Place in a clean bowl, cover with a damp cloth and leave at room temperature for 1 hour until doubled in size.

3 Preheat the oven to 220°C/425°F/Gas 7. Grease a baking sheet with dairy-free margarine. Turn the dough out again onto the floured surface and knead for about 4 minutes, then form into a ball. Flatten slightly, roll out into a large circle about 1cm/½in thick and cut with a knife to neaten. Transfer to the prepared baking sheet.

4 Make the topping by mixing together the passata and tomato purée in a bowl. Spread this mixture over the pizza base and top with the ham. Bake in the hot oven for 12–15 minutes until the base is starting to turn brown and the tomato sauce is bubbling. Take the pizza out of the oven, sprinkle the cheese shavings and rocket over the top and serve.

prawn and vegetable tempura

PREPARATION TIME **10 MINUTES** COOKING TIME **30–35 MINUTES** SERVES **4**

1 courgette, chopped into 5cm/2in batons
600g/1lb 5oz butternut or other squash, peeled, deseeded and cut into small bite-sized chunks
2 red, orange or yellow peppers, deseeded and cut into wide strips
400g/14oz asparagus, woody ends removed, trimmed to 5cm/2in
450g/1lb cooked, peeled king prawns, deveined
2 egg yolks, beaten
150g/5½oz/1⅓ cups gram flour
150g/5½oz/scant 1 cup rice flour
1 litre/1¾ pints/4 cups rapeseed or olive oil
tamari soy sauce, for dipping

1 Dry the vegetables as much as possible and drain the prawns thoroughly.
2 Mix one of the egg yolks with 185ml/6fl oz/¾ cup ice-cold water in a medium-sized mixing bowl. Sift in half of both flours, then quickly mix with a fork to blend in and make a thick but runny batter, adding another 1–2 tbsp water if needed. Do not stir too much, as the mixture should remain a little lumpy. Repeat with the other egg and remaining flours and place this second batch of batter in the fridge.
3 Pour the oil into a wok or large saucepan and place over a medium-high heat. (To test if the oil is hot enough, add a little bit of batter to it and, if the batter bobs up quickly to the surface and is sizzling, the oil is ready.)
4 Dip either a piece of vegetable or a prawn into the batter, shake it a little to remove any excess batter and then quickly slip it into the hot oil. Deep-fry the ingredients in batches of no more than 10 for 1–3 minutes until lightly golden and cooked through, depending on the ingredient – the squash will need a little longer than the other vegetables.
5 Lift out with a slotted spoon and drain on kitchen paper. Repeat with the remaining vegetables and prawns, using the second batch of batter when the first is used up. Serve immediately with the tamari soy sauce for dipping.

thai fishcakes

PREPARATION TIME **10 MINUTES** COOKING TIME **20–25 MINUTES**
ADDITIONAL TIME **MAKING THE CURRY PASTE** SERVES **4**

500g/1lb 2oz cod fillets, skinned and any remaining bones removed
1 tbsp Thai fish sauce
1 tbsp Thai Green Curry Paste (see page 20)
1 large handful chopped coriander leaves and stems
1 large egg
50g/2oz fine green beans, finely sliced
4 spring onions, finely sliced
6–8 tbsp rapeseed or olive oil

Dipping sauce:
1 tbsp Thai fish sauce
1 tbsp tamari soy sauce
juice of 1 lime
1 tbsp chopped coriander leaves

1 Place the cod, fish sauce, curry paste, coriander and egg in a liquidizer or food processor and blend thoroughly. Tip into a mixing bowl and stir in the green beans and spring onions.
2 Take about 1 tbsp of the mixture, shape it into a ball with your hands and place on a clean surface, then flatten it slightly with your palm. Repeat with the remaining mixture to make 12 fishcakes.
3 Heat 2 tbsp of the oil in a heavy-based frying pan until hot. Add three or four of the fish-cakes and cook over a medium heat for 3–4 minutes on each side until golden and crisp. Remove with a metal fish slice, drain on kitchen paper and keep warm. Repeat with the other fishcakes, adding more oil to the pan each time.
4 Meanwhile, mix all the dipping sauce ingredients together in a small serving bowl.
5 Serve the fishcakes with the dipping sauce and mixed salad leaves.

spaghetti vongole

PREPARATION TIME **5 MINUTES** COOKING TIME **8–10 MINUTES** SERVES **4**

2kg/4lb 8oz fresh clams in their shells
3 tbsp olive oil
400g/14oz gluten-free spaghetti, or other gluten-free pasta shape
4 garlic cloves, crushed
350ml/12fl oz/scant 1½ cups organic dry white wine
2 large handfuls flat-leaf parsley, coarsely chopped
sea salt and freshly ground black pepper

1. Wash the clams thoroughly under cold running water, discarding any that are open or have cracked shells.
2. Bring a large saucepan of water to the boil. Add 1 tbsp of the oil, then the spaghetti, pushing it down into the water as it softens. Cook over a medium heat for 8–10 minutes, or according to the packet instructions, stirring frequently to make sure the spaghetti doesn't stick together.
3. Meanwhile, heat the remaining oil in a large, heavy-based saucepan. Add the garlic and clams, cover the pan with a lid and leave to cook over a medium heat for 3 minutes. Pour in the wine, cover the pan and cook for 2–3 minutes until the clams have opened. Remove from the heat and discard any clams that have not opened. Stir in the chopped parsley and season lightly with salt and pepper.
4. Drain the spaghetti and rinse well with boiling water, then drain again. Tip into the pan of hot clams, stir to combine and serve immediately.

kedgeree

PREPARATION TIME **10 MINUTES** COOKING TIME **30–35 MINUTES** SERVES **4**

650g/1lb 7oz undyed smoked haddock fillets
100g/3½oz dairy-free margarine
1 onion, finely chopped
½ tbsp paprika
350g/12oz/1¾ cups long-grain rice, rinsed
2 handfuls chopped flat-leaf parsley
3 hard-boiled eggs, shelled and chopped
sea salt and freshly ground black pepper

1 Put the haddock fillets in a heavy-based saucepan, cover with 1 litre/35fl oz/4 cups boiling water, then with a lid, and simmer gently for about 10 minutes. Lift the fish out of the pan with a slotted spoon, place it on a plate and remove and discard any skin and bones. Flake the flesh with a fork. Strain and reserve the cooking liquid.

2 Melt the margarine in a large, heavy-based pan. Add the onion and cook over a medium heat for 2–3 minutes until starting to turn golden. Add the paprika and rice, then stir in the reserved cooking liquid from the haddock. Cover with a lid and bring to the boil, then turn the heat down and leave to simmer for 15–20 minutes until the rice is cooked, topping up with extra boiling water if it all gets absorbed.

3 Stir in the flaked fish and chopped parsley and continue cooking, uncovered, until all the liquid has been absorbed. Season lightly with salt and pepper and serve with the chopped eggs on top.

tomato, basil and olive penne

PREPARATION TIME **5 MINUTES** COOKING TIME **1 HOUR** SERVES **4**

16 large vine-ripened tomatoes, about 1.8kg/4lb total weight
4½ tbsp olive oil
1 large onion, chopped
2 large garlic cloves, crushed
150g/5oz/heaped 1 cup pitted black olives, cut in half
400g/14oz gluten-free penne, or other gluten-free pasta shape
4 heaped tbsp chopped basil leaves
sea salt and freshly ground black pepper

1 Preheat the oven to 180°C/350°F/Gas 4. With a sharp knife, cut a cross in the skin of each tomato, then place on a baking tray. Drizzle with 2½ tbsp of the olive oil and bake in the hot oven for 45 minutes.
2 Five minutes before the tomatoes are ready, heat 1 tbsp of the oil in a heavy-based saucepan. Add the onion and cook over a medium heat for 2–3 minutes until starting to turn golden.
3 Take the tomatoes out of the oven, remove the skins with a knife and fork and gently break up the flesh. Add the garlic to the saucepan and fry for 30 seconds, then stir in the tomato flesh along with any juices. Add the olives and season lightly with salt and pepper. Cook for 12–14 minutes until the sauce has reduced by about a half and is runny but thick.
4 Meanwhile, bring a large saucepan of water to the boil. Add the remaining oil, then the pasta, and cook over a medium heat for 8–10 minutes, or according to the packet instructions, stirring frequently to make sure the pasta doesn't stick together. Drain and rinse well with boiling water, then drain again. Tip into a large serving bowl.
5 Stir the basil into the sauce, spoon over the pasta and serve.

asparagus frittata

PREPARATION TIME **5 MINUTES** COOKING TIME **7–10 MINUTES** SERVES **2**

12 asparagus spears, woody ends removed
6 eggs
15g/½oz dairy-free margarine
50g/2oz silken tofu, finely diced
4 spring onions, finely chopped
1 tbsp chopped mint leaves
1 tbsp chopped dill
sea salt and freshly ground black pepper

1 Place the asparagus in a steamer and cook over a medium heat for 3–4 minutes until just tender but still slightly crunchy. Drain.
2 Meanwhile, beat the eggs thoroughly in a mixing bowl and add a little salt and pepper.
3 Melt the margarine in a heavy-based frying pan with an ovenproof handle over a gentle heat. Pour the egg mixture into the pan and swirl it around so that it covers the base of the pan. Quickly top with the tofu, spring onions and herbs, distributing them evenly. Finally, arrange the asparagus spears on top.
4 Preheat the grill to high. Cook the frittata on the hob for 3–4 minutes until golden on the bottom, then place the frying pan under the hot grill for 1–2 minutes until the egg mixture is cooked through and the top of the frittata is golden. Remove from the pan and place on a serving plate. Serve warm or cool, with mixed salad leaves.

spinach tart

PREPARATION TIME **15 MINUTES PLUS 30 MINUTES CHILLING TIME** COOKING TIME **40–50 MINUTES**
ADDITIONAL TIME **MAKING THE PASTRY** SERVES **4**

dairy-free margarine, for greasing
1 recipe quantity Rich Shortcrust Pastry, or gluten-free version (see page 21)
rice flour, for dusting
1 tbsp olive oil
250g/9oz baby leaf spinach
60g/2¼oz tofu
2 large eggs plus 5 large egg yolks
6 tbsp sugar-free soya milk
½ tsp freshly grated nutmeg
sea salt and freshly ground black pepper

1 Preheat the oven to 200°C/400°F/Gas 6. Grease a 25cm/10in tart tin, 3cm/1¼in deep, with dairy-free margarine.
2 Roll out the pastry on a pastry board liberally dusted with rice flour into a round about 2mm/⅛in thick and 3cm/1¼in larger all around than the tart tin, to allow enough pastry for the sides. Be careful, as the pastry will still be slightly sticky. Neaten the edge with a knife, then ease the pastry into the tin, pressing down carefully to remove any air pockets. If the dough looks too fragile to lift into the tin, simply place the tin face down on top of the pastry, then turn the board over to drop the pastry into the tin.
3 Line the pastry case with a piece of non-stick baking parchment and cover with baking beans. Bake in the hot oven for 10–12 minutes until just golden. Take the pastry case out of the oven, remove the parchment and beans and turn the oven down to 180°C/350°F/Gas 4.
4 Gently heat the olive oil in a large saucepan or wok. Add the spinach and cook over a very low heat, turning all the time, for 2–3 minutes until just wilted. Spread the spinach over the prepared pastry case, then crumble the tofu over the top. Whisk the eggs, egg yolks, soya milk and nutmeg together in a bowl, then season lightly with salt and pepper. Pour this mixture over the spinach and tofu in the pastry case.
5 Bake in the hot oven for 30–35 minutes until the filling is cooked through. Take the tart out of the oven and leave to cool in the tin until the filling has set. Carefully ease out onto a serving plate and serve with mixed salad leaves.

asparagus, oyster mushroom and sugar snap stir-fry

PREPARATION TIME **5 MINUTES** COOKING TIME **6–7 MINUTES** SERVES **4**

1 tbsp olive oil
1 tbsp sesame oil
2 bunches spring onions, finely sliced
2½cm/1in piece fresh ginger, peeled and finely chopped
½ large red chilli, deseeded and finely chopped
2 garlic cloves, crushed
500g/1lb 2oz fresh asparagus, woody ends removed, cut in half lengthways
300g/10oz sugar snap peas
250g/9oz oyster mushrooms, cut into bite-sized pieces
3 tbsp tamari soy sauce
75g/3oz/½ cup toasted sesame seeds
2 handfuls chopped coriander leaves
1 handful chopped mint leaves

1. Heat both the oils in a wok over a high heat. Add the spring onions and cook, stirring continuously, for 1 minute. Toss in the ginger, chilli and garlic, then stir in the asparagus and cook, stirring continuously, for 1 minute.
2. Add the sugar snap peas and mushrooms and leave to cook for 1 minute. Add the tamari soy sauce and stir-fry for 3–4 minutes until all the vegetables are cooked through but remain slightly crunchy.
3. Stir in the sesame seeds and the chopped herbs. Check the seasoning and add extra tamari soy sauce if needed. Serve with steamed basmati rice or rice noodles.

teas & snacks

The great news is that you don't have to go without biscuits, brownies, cookies, cakes or tarts. There are wonderful alternative ingredients that you can use, including soya products, rice and gram flour and ground almonds. And here you'll find a mouth-watering collection of recipes using these ingredients. Baking is pure comfort food – in the making as well as the eating. All you need are a few baking trays, some ingredients and a little bit of time. Most of the bakes in this chapter will keep for a few days, so you can make them at the weekend and munch through them during the week. Whether it's rich Chocolate and Hazlenut Brownies, tangy Lemon Polenta Cake, creamy Fruit Tarts or crunchy Sunflower Seed Biscuits, here are gorgeous treats for you to enjoy and, if they really insist, to share with family and friends!

chocolate and hazlenut brownies

PREPARATION TIME **10 MINUTES** COOKING TIME **12–15 MINUTES** MAKES **20**

150g/5oz dairy-free margarine, plus extra for greasing
200g/7oz dairy-free dark chocolate, with at least 70 per cent cocoa solids
200g/7oz/1 cup fruit sugar
2 large eggs, beaten
1 tsp vanilla essence
50g/2oz/scant 1/3 cup rice flour
25g/1oz/scant 1/4 cup gram flour
1 tsp gluten-free baking powder
100g/3 1/2oz/heaped 3/4 cup chopped hazelnuts

1 Preheat the oven to 180°C/350°F/Gas 4. Grease a 20 x 30cm/8 x 12in baking tin with dairy-free margarine and line the base with non-stick baking parchment.
2 Break the chocolate into small pieces and place in a large heatproof bowl. Rest the bowl over a pan of gently simmering water, making sure that the bottom of the bowl does not touch the water. Stir from time to time until the chocolate has melted. Add the margarine to the bowl and continue stirring occasionally until it is completely melted and mixed in with the chocolate.
3 Remove the bowl from the heat and stir in the sugar, followed by the beaten eggs and vanilla essence. Stir to mix well, then sift the flours and baking powder into the bowl and carefully fold in with a metal spoon, making sure the mixture is thoroughly combined but not stirred too heavily, or the air will be lost. Fold in the nuts.
4 Spoon the mixture into the prepared tin, spreading it evenly into the corners with the back of the spoon. Bake in the hot oven for 12–15 minutes until risen and firm to the touch and a skewer inserted in the centre has just a little mixture sticking to it. Remove from the oven and leave to cool in the tin for 5 minutes, then transfer to a wire rack and leave to cool completely. Cut into 20 squares.

fig and pecan nut crunchies

PREPARATION TIME **10 MINUTES** COOKING TIME **20–22 MINUTES** MAKES **10**

150g/5oz dairy-free margarine, plus extra for greasing
75g/2½oz/scant ½ cup fruit sugar
1 tbsp clear honey
1 tsp freshly grated nutmeg
30g/1¼oz/⅓ cup barley flour
60g/2¼oz/heaped ½ cup gram flour
60g/2¼oz/⅓ cup rice flour
1 tsp baking powder
150g/5oz/1½ cups jumbo oats
150g/5oz sugar-free dried figs, chopped
50g/2oz pecan nuts, chopped

1. Preheat the oven to 180°C/350°F/Gas 4 and lightly grease a baking tray with dairy-free margarine. Place the margarine, sugar and honey in a saucepan and heat gently until the margarine has melted and the sugar has dissolved. Stir in the nutmeg.
2. Sift the flours with the baking powder into a large mixing bowl. Add the oats, figs and pecan nuts and mix well. Pour in the melted margarine mixture and mix together thoroughly.
3. Take 2 tbsp of the mixture and shape into a ball with your hands. Place on the prepared baking tray, spaced well apart. Repeat until you have used up all the mixture, then flatten each ball slightly with the palm of your hand.
4. Bake in the hot oven for 20–22 minutes until golden brown. Take the crunchies out of the oven, transfer to a wire rack and leave to cool completely.

almond biscuits

PREPARATION TIME **10 MINUTES** COOKING TIME **14–17 MINUTES** MAKES **14–16**

175g/6oz dairy-free margarine
40g/1¾oz/scant ¼ cup fruit sugar
135g/4½oz/¾ cup rice flour
40g/1¾oz/heaped ⅓ cup gram flour
30g/1oz/scant ⅓ cup ground almonds
scant ½ tsp almond essence

1 Preheat the oven to 180°C/350°F/Gas 4. Lay sheets of non-stick baking parchment on two baking trays.

2 Place the margarine and sugar in a saucepan and heat gently until the margarine has melted and the sugar has dissolved. Bring to the boil, then turn the heat down and leave to simmer for 4–5 minutes until the mixture has caramelized slightly and become syrupy.

3 Sift the flours and ground almonds into a large mixing bowl. Pour in the sugar mixture, add the almond essence and stir thoroughly with a wooden spoon until mixed.

4 Spoon the mixture, 1 tbsp at a time, onto the prepared baking trays to form 14–16 balls. Press down on each ball with the back of the spoon to make a biscuit shape.

5 Bake in the hot oven for 10–12 minutes until lightly browned. Take the biscuits out of the oven and leave to cool for 5 minutes, then transfer to a wire rack and leave to cool completely.

lemon polenta cake

PREPARATION TIME **10 MINUTES** COOKING TIME **35–40 MINUTES** SERVES **10**

300g/10oz dairy-free margarine, softened, plus extra for greasing
200g/7oz/1 cup fruit sugar
4 large eggs, beaten
4 tbsp clear honey
350g/12oz/2⅓ cups quick-cook polenta
100g/3½oz/1 cup ground almonds, plus extra for topping
1 tsp gluten-free baking powder
juice of 1½ lemons and grated zest of 1 lemon, plus pared or grated zest of another lemon to decorate

1. Preheat the oven to 180°C/350°F/Gas 4. Lightly grease a deep 20cm/8in cake tin with dairy-free margarine and line the base with a circle of non-stick baking parchment.
2. Using a hand-held electric whisk, beat the margarine and sugar together in a large mixing bowl until light and fluffy. Gradually beat in the eggs, a little at a time, then the honey.
3. Using a metal spoon, fold in the polenta, ground almonds and baking powder, then the lemon juice and zest. Mix thoroughly and pour into the prepared cake tin.
4. Bake in the oven for 35–40 minutes until golden brown around the sides and firm to the touch and a skewer inserted in the centre comes out clean. You will notice that there are cracks all over the top. Take the cake out of the oven and leave to cool in the tin for 5 minutes, then turn out onto a wire rack and leave to cool completely.
5. Sprinkle with the extra ground almonds and the pared or grated lemon zest.

spicy gingerbread

PREPARATION TIME **10 MINUTES** COOKING TIME **20–25 MINUTES** SERVES **8**

100g/3½oz dairy-free margarine, softened, plus extra for greasing
75g/2½oz/scant ½ cup fruit sugar
1 egg, beaten
3 tbsp date syrup
100g/3½oz/heaped ½ cup rice flour
50g/2oz/scant ½ cup gram flour
50g/2oz/scant ⅓ cup millet flour
2 tsp ground ginger
2cm/¾in piece fresh ginger, peeled and finely chopped

1. Preheat the oven to 180°C/350°F/Gas 4. Lightly grease a deep 20cm/8in cake tin with dairy-free margarine and line the base with a circle of non-stick baking parchment.
2. Using a hand-held electric whisk, beat the margarine and sugar together in a large mixing bowl until light and fluffy. Gradually beat in the egg, a little at a time, then the date syrup.
3. Sift in the flours and add the ground and fresh ginger. Fold in with a metal spoon until thoroughly mixed.
4. Tip the mixture into the prepared cake tin and bake in the hot oven for 20–25 minutes until it is a rich golden brown and a skewer inserted into the centre comes out with just a little of the mixture sticking to it. Take the gingerbread out of the oven, leave to cool in the tin for 3–4 minutes, then turn out onto a wire rack and leave to cool completely before serving.

banana bread

PREPARATION TIME **10 MINUTES** COOKING TIME **45–50 MINUTES** SERVES **6**

100g/$3\frac{1}{2}$oz dairy-free margarine, softened, plus extra for greasing
100g/$3\frac{1}{2}$oz/heaped $\frac{1}{2}$ cup fruit sugar
2 large eggs
1 tsp vanilla essence
80g/$2\frac{3}{4}$oz/scant $\frac{1}{2}$ cup rice flour
40g/$1\frac{3}{4}$oz/scant $\frac{1}{4}$ cup millet flour
40g/$1\frac{3}{4}$oz/heaped $\frac{1}{3}$ cup gram flour
2 tsp gluten-free baking powder
4 very ripe bananas, mashed

1. Preheat the oven to 180°C/350°F/Gas 4. Grease a 450g/1lb loaf tin with dairy-free margarine.
2. Using a hand-held electric whisk, beat the margarine and sugar together in a large mixing bowl until light and fluffy. Gradually beat in the eggs, a little at a time, then the vanilla essence.
3. Sift the flours and baking powder into a clean bowl. With a metal spoon, carefully fold half the flour into the mixture, then repeat with the remaining flour. Add the bananas and fold in until thoroughly mixed in.
4. Spoon the mixture into the prepared tin and bake in the hot oven for 45–50 minutes until a rich golden brown on top and firm to the touch. When the banana bread is cooked, a skewer inserted in the centre should come out with just a smear of mixture on it. Take the banana bread out of the oven, leave to cool in the tin for 3–4 minutes, then turn out onto a wire rack and leave to cool completely before serving.

carrot and beetroot cupcakes

PREPARATION TIME **10 MINUTES** COOKING TIME **15–20 MINUTES** MAKES **10**

150g/5oz dairy-free margarine, softened
125g/4oz/¾ cup fruit sugar
3 eggs, beaten
75g/2½oz/scant ½ cup rice flour
75g/2½oz/⅔ cup gram flour
1 tsp gluten-free baking powder
1 tsp bicarbonate of soda
1 tsp ground cinnamon
200g/7oz carrots, peeled and grated
100g/3½oz beetroots, peeled and grated

Topping:
100g/3½oz soya yogurt
2 tbsp clear honey

1 Preheat the oven to 180°C/350°F/Gas 4. Arrange 10 paper cupcake cases in a muffin tin.
2 Using a hand-held electric whisk, beat the margarine and sugar together in a large mixing bowl until light and fluffy. Gradually beat in the eggs, a little at a time, until well mixed.
3 Sift the flours, baking powder, bicarbonate of soda and ground cinnamon into the mixture, then quickly fold it in, followed by the grated carrots and beetroots, using a metal spoon. Make sure the mixture is well blended, but take care not to overmix.
4 Divide the mixture between the cupcake cases and bake in the hot oven for 10 minutes, then cover them with a sheet of non-stick baking parchment to prevent them from over-browning and bake for a further 5–10 minutes until well risen and a skewer inserted in the centre comes out clean. Take the cupcakes out of the oven, transfer to a wire rack and leave to cool completely.
5 When the cupcakes have cooled, prepare the topping. Using a whisk or hand-held electric blender, whisk together the yogurt and honey in a bowl until smooth. Spread a little of the topping over each one.

apricot, mango and coconut bars

PREPARATION TIME **10 MINUTES** COOKING TIME **45–50 MINUTES** MAKES **10**

dairy-free margarine, for greasing
100g/3½oz sugar-free dried unsulphured apricots, finely chopped
100g/3½oz sugar-free dried mango, finely chopped
35g/1½oz/⅔ cup unsweetened coconut flakes
200g/7oz creamed coconut
200g/7oz/2 cups porridge oats
2 tbsp olive oil
4 tbsp mango or date syrup

1 Preheat the oven to 180°C/350°F/Gas 4. Grease a 20 x 30cm/8 x 12in baking tin with dairy-free margarine and line the base with non-stick baking parchment.

2 Put the dried apricots and mango in a saucepan with 500ml/17fl oz/2 cups water. Bring to the boil, then turn the heat down and leave to simmer for 15–20 minutes until the fruit has softened and the water has been absorbed.

3 Meanwhile, heat a heavy-based frying pan over a medium heat until hot. Toss in the coconut flakes and dry-fry until lightly browned, turning frequently to prevent burning. Tip the coconut into a bowl. Melt the creamed coconut in a small saucepan over a very low heat.

4 Place the oats in a large mixing bowl and make a well in the middle. Pour in the oil and work it into the oats with your fingertips, ensuring the oil is evenly distributed. Stir in the melted creamed coconut, the mango or date syrup and half the soft apricot and mango mixture, mixing thoroughly.

5 Spread half the oat mixture in a thin layer over the bottom of the prepared baking tin, pressing down firmly with your fingertips or the back of a metal spoon. Spread the remaining apricot and mango mixture over the top, then spread the remaining oat mixture on top of that to create a layered traybake.

6 Bake in the hot oven for 25–30 minutes until golden brown and firm. Remove from the oven, sprinkle the coconut flakes over the top and leave to cool in the tin for 3–4 minutes. Cut into 10 bars, remove from the tin and leave to cool completely on a wire rack before serving.

raspberry tarts

PREPARATION TIME **15 MINUTES** COOKING TIME **35–40 MINUTES**
ADDITIONAL TIME **MAKING THE PASTRY** MAKES **6**

90g/3¼oz dairy-free margarine, softened, plus extra for greasing
1 recipe quantity Sweet Rich Shortcrust Pastry (see page 22)
rice flour, for dusting
50g/2oz/¼ cup fruit sugar, plus extra for dusting
1 large egg, beaten
100g/3½oz/1 cup ground almonds
200g/7oz fresh raspberries

1 Preheat the oven to 190°C/375°F/Gas 5. Grease a six-hole muffin tray with dairy-free margarine.
2 Gently roll out the pastry on a surface lightly dusted with rice flour until about 2mm/⅛in thick. Using a pastry cutter that is slightly larger in diameter than the muffin holes, cut out six pastry circles. Be very gentle, as the dough will still be slightly sticky.
3 Lift the pastry circles into the muffin holes (you may need to use a palette knife) and press down lightly to remove any pockets of air. Line each pastry case with a piece of non-stick baking parchment and cover with baking beans. Bake in the hot oven for 8–10 minutes until firm and lightly golden.
4 Meanwhile, using a hand-held electric whisk, beat the margarine and sugar together in a large mixing bowl until light and fluffy. Gradually beat in the egg, a little at a time, until well mixed, then fold in the ground almonds.
5 Take the pastry cases out of the oven and remove the parchment and beans. Spoon the prepared filling mixture into the pastry cases. Press a small handful of raspberries into each tart and return to the hot oven for 25–30 minutes until firm and golden brown. Take the tarts out of the oven, allow to cool in the tin for 5 minutes, then transfer to a wire rack to cool completely. Grind the extra sugar with a hand-held electric mini-blender or a pestle and mortar and sprinkle over the tarts before serving.

fruit tarts

PREPARATION TIME **20 MINUTES** COOKING TIME **25 MINUTES**
ADDITIONAL TIME **MAKING THE PASTRY** MAKES **4 OR 6**

dairy-free margarine, for greasing
1 recipe quantity Sweet Rich Shortcrust Pastry (see page 22)
rice flour, for dusting
250ml/9fl oz/1 cup soya milk
1½ tsp cornflour
3 large egg yolks
40g/1¾oz/¼ cup fruit sugar
½ tsp vanilla essence
9–15 strawberries, depending on size, hulled and cut in half, or 3 peaches or nectarines, peeled, pitted and sliced lengthways into eight pieces
1 tbsp sugar-free apricot jam

1 Preheat the oven to 200°C/400°F/Gas 6. Grease 1½ x four-hole Yorkshire pudding tins or 4 x 12cm/5in tartlet tins, 2cm/¾in deep, with dairy-free margarine.
2 Gently roll out the pastry on a surface liberally dusted with rice flour until about 2mm/⅛in thick. Using a pastry cutter that is slightly larger in diameter than the Yorkshire pudding tin holes or the tartlet tins, to allow enough pastry for the sides, cut out six or four pastry circles, discarding any extra pastry. Be very gentle, as the dough will still be slightly sticky.
3 Lift the pastry circles into each hole or tin (you may need to use a metal spatula) and press down lightly to remove any pockets of air. Line each pastry case with a piece of non-stick baking parchment and cover with baking beans. Place the tartlet tins, if using, on a baking tray. Bake in the hot oven for 8–10 minutes until firm and lightly golden.
4 Meanwhile, heat the soya milk in a heavy-based saucepan over a low heat until almost boiling. In a small bowl, mix 1 tsp water into the cornflour. Whisk the egg yolks in a large bowl for 2 minutes, add the sugar and the cornflour mixture and whisk for another 2–3 minutes until thick. Pour in the warm milk and add the vanilla essence, stirring well. Pour the sauce back into the pan and heat gently for 5–10 minutes, stirring or whisking, until thick and creamy.
5 Take the pastry cases out of the oven and remove the parchment and beans. Turn the oven down to 180°C/350°F/Gas 4. Divide the custard between the cases, arrange 3–5 strawberry halves or 4 peach or nectarine slices on each one and bake for 15 minutes. Take the tarts out of the oven, leave to cool, then remove from the tins.
6 Gently heat the apricot jam with about 1 tsp water in a small saucepan until the jam has dissolved. Brush the tops of the fruit lightly with this glaze, using a pastry brush, and serve.

sunflower seed biscuits

PREPARATION TIME **10 MINUTES** COOKING TIME **30 MINUTES** MAKES **8**

50g/2oz dairy-free margarine, plus extra for greasing
50g/2oz/heaped 1/3 cup sunflower seeds
200g/7oz/scant 2 cups gram flour
200g/7oz/scant 1 1/4 cups rice flour, plus extra for dusting
1 1/2 tsp gluten-free baking powder
1/2 tsp salt
3 tbsp olive oil

1 Preheat the oven to 180°C/350°F/Gas 4. Grease two baking trays with dairy-free margarine.
2 Place the sunflower seeds in a heavy-based frying pan over a medium heat and dry-fry until just beginning to brown. Remove from the pan.
3 Sift the flours, baking powder and salt into a large mixing bowl. Make a well in the centre and pour in the oil. With your fingertips, rub the oil into the flour mixture. Add the margarine and, using your fingertips, rub in until thoroughly mixed. Stir in the toasted sunflower seeds.
4 Make a well in the flour mixture and pour in 165ml/5 1/2fl oz/2/3 cup water. Gradually mix in until well blended. Bring together to form a ball of soft dough.
5 Turn out onto a surface liberally dusted with rice flour and roll out the dough until about 5mm/1/4in thick. Using a 12cm/5in pastry cutter, cut out eight circles of dough. You'll need to keep shaping the dough into a ball and then rolling it out again with the rolling pin in order to cut all the circles. Place on the prepared baking trays and bake in the hot oven for 28–30 minutes until golden brown.
6 Take the biscuits out of the oven, leave to cool in the tins for 3–4 minutes, then transfer to a wire rack and leave to cool completely before serving with dairy-free cheese, Avocado Salsa (see page 64) or Smoked Salmon Pâté (see page 42).

sun-dried tomato oatcakes

PREPARATION TIME **10 MINUTES** COOKING TIME **20–25 MINUTES** MAKES **8**

30g/1¼oz dairy-free margarine, plus extra for greasing
250g/9oz/2 cups fine oatmeal
½ tsp bicarbonate of soda
½ tsp dried oregano
75g/2½oz sun-dried tomatoes in oil, drained and chopped

1 Preheat the oven to 200°C/400°F/Gas 6. Grease 2 x four-hole Yorkshire pudding tins or 8 x 12cm/5in tartlet tins, 2cm/¾in deep, with dairy-free margarine.

2 Mix together the oatmeal, bicarbonate of soda and oregano in a large mixing bowl and make a well in the centre. Melt the margarine in a saucepan over a low heat and pour into the well. With a wooden spoon, gradually mix the melted margarine into the oatmeal mixture, ensuring it is evenly distributed. Add the sun-dried tomatoes and 100ml/3½fl oz/scant ½ cup water and mix until well combined.

3 Divide the mixture into eight and press one portion into the base of each prepared hole or tartlet tin. You may find the back of a metal spoon works better than your fingers, as the mixture is quite sticky. If using tartlet tins, place them on a baking tray.

4 Bake in the hot oven for 20–25 minutes until golden brown. Take the oatcakes out of the oven, leave to cool in the tins for 5 minutes, then turn out onto a wire rack and leave to cool completely before serving with dairy-free cheese, hummus or Artichoke Pâté (see page 45).

dinners

If you thought you couldn't have risotto any longer, or pasta or curry, think again. This chapter is packed with mouth-watering main courses, many of which you'll be amazed to find you can eat. Delicious Gnocchi with Mushroom and Pancetta Sauce will provide a substantial, warming meal, and Salmon Fishcakes, with their crunchy coating, will be a hit with your kids. Choose from a range of quick suppers that can be whipped up in less than 30 minutes, such as Pork with Chestnuts, Apple and Sage, much-loved family favourites, such as Spaghetti with Meatballs, or indulgent meals for a special occasion, such as Duck with Cherry and Juniper Sauce or Herbed Monkfish Wrapped in Parma Ham. This is food for everyone – for sharing good times together.

chicken farci with pea and mint purée

PREPARATION TIME **10 MINUTES, PLUS 2 HOURS MARINATING TIME** COOKING TIME **35 MINUTES**
ADDITIONAL TIME **MAKING THE STOCK** SERVES **4**

4 skinless, boneless chicken breasts
8 tbsp olive oil
juice of 1 lime
2 shallots, finely chopped
500g/1lb 2oz peas in their pods, shelled (200g/7oz/1¼ heaped cups shelled)
200ml/7fl oz/generous ¾ cup Vegetable Stock (see page 25), or stock made from gluten-, yeast- and dairy-free stock powder
2 heaped tbsp chopped mint leaves
25g/1oz silken tofu, chopped
sea salt and freshly ground black pepper

1 Arrange the chicken breasts in a large dish. Mix 6 tbsp of the oil with the lime juice in a small jug, then pour over the chicken. Cover and leave in the fridge to marinate for 2 hours.

2 Preheat the oven to 180°C/350°F/Gas 4. Heat the remaining oil in a heavy-based saucepan, add the shallots and fry over a low heat for 1–2 minutes. Add the peas and stock and cook for 5 minutes. Stir in the mint, then season lightly with salt and pepper.

3 Add the tofu to the saucepan, then blend with a hand-held electric blender. Alternatively, blend the mixture in a liquidizer or food processor. Pour the mixture into a sieve set over a bowl and work it through with a wooden spoon to form a smooth purée, reserving the liquid.

4 Remove the chicken from the dish, discarding the marinade. Make a long horizontal slit through the thickest part of each breast without cutting right through, to create a pocket. Stuff as much purée as you can into each pocket, then close up the opening with wooden cocktail sticks.

5 Place the stuffed chicken breasts in an ovenproof dish and spread the remaining purée over the top of each breast. Pour the reserved liquid onto the base of the dish, taking care not to pour it onto the chicken. Bake in the hot oven for 25 minutes until the chicken is cooked through. Remove the cocktail sticks and serve with boiled new potatoes and vegetables.

chicken and herb risotto

PREPARATION TIME **5 MINUTES** COOKING TIME **25–30 MINUTES**
ADDITIONAL TIME **MAKING THE STOCK** SERVES **4**

800ml/1½ pints/scant 3½ cups Chicken or Vegetable Stock (see pages 24–5), or vegetable stock made from gluten-, yeast- and dairy-free stock powder
6 tbsp olive oil
4 skinless, boneless chicken breasts, cut into bite-sized pieces
1 small onion, finely chopped
2 tbsp chopped flat-leaf parsley
2 tbsp chopped mint leaves
2 tbsp chopped basil leaves
250g/9oz/heaped 1 cup arborio or other risotto rice
300ml/10fl oz/scant 1¼ cups organic dry white wine
sea salt and freshly ground black pepper

1 Heat the stock in a saucepan until almost boiling, then turn the heat down, cover with a lid and leave to simmer while you prepare the rice mixture.
2 Heat 2 tbsp of the oil in a large, heavy-based saucepan. Add the chicken and cook over a medium heat for 5–6 minutes until lightly browned. Remove from the pan with a slotted spoon and leave to one side.
3 Put the remaining oil in the pan and heat until hot. Add the onion and cook on a medium heat for 2–3 minutes until starting to turn golden, then stir in half of the chopped herbs. Add the rice and stir thoroughly so that each grain is coated with oil.
4 Pour a little of the wine into the mixture and stir. Continue cooking over a low heat, gradually adding and stirring in the wine, until it has all been absorbed. Add the chicken and a ladle of the simmering stock and stir until all the liquid has been absorbed. Continue adding stock and stirring for about 18–20 minutes until the rice is just tender but still has a little bite and all the liquid has been absorbed.
5 Stir in the remaining herbs and season lightly with salt and pepper. Serve with mixed salad leaves.

chicken with salsa verde

PREPARATION TIME **10 MINUTES** COOKING TIME **10–12 MINUTES** SERVES **4**

1 tbsp olive oil
4 skinless, boneless chicken breasts
350g/12oz green beans, trimmed
500g/1lb 2oz baby leaf spinach

Salsa verde:
2 heaped tbsp chopped basil leaves
2 heaped tbsp chopped mint leaves
2 heaped tbsp chopped flat-leaf parsley
1 garlic clove, chopped
6 anchovies in oil, drained and chopped
2 tbsp capers in brine, rinsed
juice of $^1/_2$ lemon
2 tbsp olive oil

1. Make the salsa verde by putting the herbs, garlic, anchovies and capers into a food processor and blending to form a paste. With the motor running, gradually pour in the lemon juice and the oil until well combined. Transfer to a bowl and cover.
2. Heat the oil in a large, heavy-based saucepan, add the chicken, cover with a lid and cook over a medium heat, turning occasionally, for 10–12 minutes until cooked through.
3. About halfway through the cooking time, place the beans in a steamer and steam for 2 minutes. Add the spinach and continue cooking for another minute until the beans are just tender and the spinach is beginning to wilt.
4. Spread the salsa verde over the chicken pieces and serve with the beans and spinach and with fried or grilled slices of Quick Polenta (see page 143) and mixed salad leaves.

thai-style green chicken curry

PREPARATION TIME **10 MINUTES** COOKING TIME **20–25 MINUTES**
ADDITIONAL TIME **MAKING THE CURRY PASTE** SERVES **4**

2 tbsp olive oil
4 skinless, boneless chicken breasts, cut into thin strips
400ml/14fl oz/1²/₃-cup tin coconut milk
2 tbsp Thai Green Curry Paste (see page 20)
3 tbsp Thai fish sauce
4 kaffir lime leaves, or a strip of lime peel
100g/3¹/₂oz green beans, trimmed
1 red or yellow pepper, deseeded and cut into thin strips
100g/3¹/₂oz sugar snap peas
100g/3¹/₂oz beansprouts
1 small handful sweet basil leaves, cut in half
¹/₂ large green chilli, deseeded and cut into fine strips
1 large handful coriander leaves

1 Heat a wok until hot, pour in the oil and swirl it around. Add the chicken and cook over a medium heat, stirring continuously, for 2–3 minutes until lightly browned, then remove and put on a plate. Pour the coconut milk into the wok and cook gently for 4–5 minutes. Add the curry paste and cook for 2–3 minutes, stirring well.
2 Add the fish sauce, lime leaves or strip of lime peel, green beans and pepper and cook gently for 3–4 minutes. Take care not to let it boil or the coconut milk will curdle. Add the sugar snap peas and beansprouts and cook for 10 minutes until the chicken is cooked.
3 Check the seasoning and add a little more fish sauce if desired. Sprinkle with the basil, chilli and coriander and serve with steamed basmati rice.

tender roast chicken

PREPARATION TIME **10 MINUTES** COOKING TIME **1¾ HOURS**
ADDITIONAL TIME **MAKING THE STOCK** SERVES **4**

1.8kg/4lb chicken
1 tbsp olive oil
1 large garlic clove, sliced
4 rosemary sprigs
800g/1lb 12oz potatoes, peeled and cut into quarters
250ml/9fl oz/1 cup Chicken or Vegetable Stock (see pages 24–5), or vegetable stock made from gluten-, yeast- and dairy-free stock powder
250ml/9fl oz/1 cup organic dry white wine
sea salt and freshly ground black pepper

1 Preheat the oven to 180°C/350°F/Gas 4. Place the chicken in a large ovenproof dish and rub the oil over it. With a sharp knife, make incisions in the flesh along the breast and top of the thighs. Insert a slice of garlic into each incision, pushing it down into the flesh. Lay the rosemary sprigs over the top of the chicken.

2 Arrange the potatoes around the sides of the chicken and season both the chicken and potatoes lightly with salt and pepper. Pour the stock and wine into the base of the dish and cover the dish with greaseproof paper, ensuring the ends of the paper are tucked under the dish.

3 Roast in the hot oven for 1 hour. Remove the greaseproof paper and leave to one side. Cook for a further 40 minutes until the juices from the chicken run clear when the thickest part of the thigh is pierced with a skewer. If the juices look at all pink, cook for a little longer. Take the chicken and potatoes out of the oven and replace the greaseproof paper, ensuring the ends of the paper are tucked under the dish, and leave to stand in a warm place for 10–15 minutes.

4 Meanwhile, tip the cooking juices into a jug and, using a spoon, remove and discard the layer of fat that will rise to the surface. Pour the juices into a saucepan and cook over a high heat for 2–3 minutes to reduce. Serve with the chicken and potatoes along with Roasted Vegetables (see page 145), Italian-style Vegetables (see page 148) or Red Cabbage and Apple (see page 147).

confit of duck

PREPARATION TIME **15 MINUTES, PLUS 2 DAYS CHILLING TIME**
COOKING TIME **2 HOURS** SERVES **4**

4 large duck legs
25g/1oz sea salt
2 garlic cloves, crushed
6 thyme sprigs
1kg/2lb 4oz goose or duck fat

1 Arrange the duck legs, skin-side up, in an ovenproof dish just large enough to hold them. Sprinkle over the salt and garlic and place the sprigs of thyme on top. Cover with a lid and leave in the fridge for 24 hours. Do not leave any longer, as the duck will become too salty.

2 Take the duck out of the dish and wipe thoroughly with kitchen paper to remove all the salt. Clean the dish and arrange the duck legs in it as before. Preheat the oven to 140°C/275°F/ Gas 1.

3 Heat the goose or duck fat in a saucepan over a low heat until starting to bubble, then pour it into the dish, covering all the duck pieces. Cover and cook in the warm oven for $1\frac{1}{2}$ hours. Take the duck out of the oven and leave to cool.

4 Take the cooled duck legs out of the dish and put on a plate. Pour the remaining fat through a sieve into a bowl and discard any meat juices that are left on the bottom of the dish. Clean the dish and return the duck legs to it. Pour over the strained fat, cover the dish and leave to chill in the fridge for 24 hours.

5 Preheat the oven to 180°C/350°F/Gas 4. Remove the duck from the dish and wipe off most of the fat. Place the duck on a rack above a roasting tin and cook in the hot oven for 20 minutes until the skin is crisp and golden and the meat is cooked through. Take the duck out of the oven and serve with Red Cabbage and Apple (see page 147) and Potatoes with Porcini Mushrooms (see page 142).

duck with cherry and juniper sauce

PREPARATION TIME **10 MINUTES** COOKING TIME **25–35 MINUTES** SERVES **4**

450g/1lb cherries, cut in half and pitted
5 juniper berries, crushed
175ml/6fl oz/$^{2}/_{3}$ cup organic red wine
4 duck breasts
$^{1}/_{2}$ tsp sea salt
1 tbsp olive oil
1 tsp cornflour
2–3 tsp sugar-free cherry jam

1 Preheat the oven to 180°C/350°F/Gas 4. Place the cherries and juniper berries in a saucepan with the red wine. Bring to the boil over a medium heat, then turn the heat down, cover with a lid and leave to simmer for 10–15 minutes until the cherries have softened, crushing them from time to time with the back of a wooden spoon.

2 Meanwhile, slash the skin of each duck breast and sprinkle the salt over them. Heat the oil in a heavy-based frying pan. Add the duck, skin-side down, and cook over a medium-high heat for 4–5 minutes until the skin is browned. Using a slotted spoon, lift the duck breasts from the pan and arrange in a roasting tin, skin-side up. Pour the juices from the pan over the top. Cook the duck in the hot oven for 20–25 minutes until the skin is crisp but the meat is still slightly pink in the middle.

3 When the cherries have softened, remove from the heat and pour the mixture through a non-metallic sieve set over a bowl, using the back of a metal spoon to push as much of the liquid through as possible. Discard the contents of the sieve. Rinse the saucepan, pour the liquid back into it and return to the heat. Bring to the boil, then turn the heat down and leave to simmer for 15–20 minutes, stirring occasionally, until reduced by half.

4 Mix 1 tsp water with the cornflour in a small bowl to make a smooth paste. Stir into the simmering cherry and juniper liquid and continue to simmer for a further 4–5 minutes, stirring occasionally, until the sauce has thickened. Stir in the jam to taste.

5 When the duck has cooked, take it out of the oven and serve with the sauce, Olive Oil Herb Mash (see page 141) and vegetables.

pork with chestnuts, apple and sage

PREPARATION TIME **10 MINUTES** COOKING TIME **12–15 MINUTES** SERVES **4**

2 tbsp olive oil
1 red onion, sliced lengthways into 16 pieces
1 garlic clove, crushed
650g/1lb 7oz pork tenderloin, trimmed of fat and cut into bite-sized chunks
100g/3½oz cooked, peeled chestnuts (fresh or vacuum-packed), cut into thirds
2 eating apples, peeled, quartered and cored, and sliced lengthways into 16 pieces
1 heaped tbsp chopped sage leaves
sea salt and freshly ground black pepper

1 Heat the oil in a large, heavy-based saucepan. Add the onion and fry over a gentle heat for 2 minutes until just starting to turn golden. Stir in the garlic and then the pork, cover with a lid and cook for 5 minutes, shaking the pan occasionally to turn the pork.
2 Remove the lid, add the chestnuts, apples and sage and cook for 5–8 minutes until the apple is soft and the liquid has evaporated. Season lightly with salt and pepper and serve the pork with Herb Mash (see page 141) made with a small handful sage instead of the parsley or coriander and vegetables.

pork with umeboshi sauce

PREPARATION TIME **5 MINUTES** COOKING TIME **11–13 MINUTES** SERVES **4**

4 tbsp olive oil

650g/1lb 7oz pork tenderloin, trimmed of fat and sliced into 2cm/¾in rounds

2 bunches spring onions, finely sliced

Umeboshi sauce:

150ml/5fl oz/scant ⅔ cup clear honey

2 tbsp umeboshi paste

2 tbsp tamari soy sauce

1 tsp Chinese five-spice powder

1. Mix together the sauce ingredients in a jug or bowl until well blended.
2. Heat the oil in a large wok, add the pork and stir-fry over a high heat for 5–6 minutes, stirring continuously. Add the spring onions and stir-fry for 1 minute.
3. Pour the umeboshi sauce over and cook for 5–6 minutes, stirring occasionally, until the pork is cooked through and the sauce has reduced a little. Serve with steamed rice.

gnocchi with mushroom and pancetta sauce

PREPARATION TIME **20 MINUTES** COOKING TIME **25–30 MINUTES**
ADDITIONAL TIME **MAKING THE SAUCE** SERVES **4**

2 tbsp olive oil
1 onion, finely chopped
2 garlic cloves, crushed
350g/12oz nitrate-free pancetta, chopped
300g/10oz mushrooms, sliced
1 recipe quantity White Wine Sauce (see page 19)
sea salt and freshly ground black pepper

Gnocchi:
750g/1lb 9oz potatoes, peeled and cut into large chunks
3 egg yolks, beaten
125g/4oz/scant 3/4 cup rice flour, plus extra for dusting
sea salt and freshly ground black pepper

1 To make the gnocchi, put the potatoes in a saucepan and cover with cold water. Place over a high heat, bring to the boil, then turn the heat down, cover with a lid and leave to simmer for 15–20 minutes until tender. Meanwhile, heat the oil for the sauce in a heavy-based frying pan. Add the onion and cook over a medium heat for 2–3 minutes until starting to turn golden. Stir in the garlic, then add the pancetta and fry for 3–4 minutes. Add the mushrooms and cook for 10 minutes, stirring occasionally.
2 When the potatoes are cooked, drain and mash well, then warm over a low heat for a few minutes. Tip into a large bowl, season lightly with salt and pepper, then beat in the egg yolks and flour, a little at a time, with a wooden spoon to form a smooth, slightly sticky dough.
3 Turn the dough out onto a surface dusted with rice flour and, with floured hands, knead and work it into a ball. Roll out to form into a long sausage about 2cm/3/4in in diameter. Cut into 2cm/3/4in lengths, then use the back of a fork to make grooves across the top of each piece. Leave on the floured surface, making sure they do not overlap.
4 Fill a large pan with boiling water and set over a medium heat so that the water simmers gently. Add a third of the prepared gnocchi and cook until they rise to the surface. Continue cooking for another 1–2 minutes, then remove with a slotted spoon and keep warm. Repeat with the remaining gnocchi.
5 Meanwhile, heat the white wine sauce over a gentle heat until almost boiling. Stir in the pancetta mixture and season lightly with salt and pepper. Pour the sauce over the gnocchi and serve.

roasted squash, leek and bacon risotto

PREPARATION TIME **5 MINUTES** COOKING TIME **45 MINUTES**
ADDITIONAL TIME **MAKING THE STOCK** SERVES **4**

1kg/2lb 4oz butternut or other squash, peeled, deseeded and cut into bite-sized pieces
3 tbsp olive oil
1 litre/1¾ pints/4 cups Chicken or Vegetable Stock (see pages 24–5), or vegetable stock made from gluten-, yeast- and dairy-free stock powder
1 small onion, finely chopped
2 garlic cloves, crushed
3 leeks, about 400g/14oz total weight, trimmed and sliced
6 rashers rindless nitrate-free back bacon, about 200g/7oz total weight, diced
250g/9oz/heaped 1 cup arborio or other risotto rice
sea salt and freshly ground black pepper

1. Preheat the oven to 180°C/350°F/Gas 4. Place the squash in a roasting tin, drizzle over 2 tbsp of the oil and roast in the hot oven for 45 minutes, until tender.
2. When the squash has been roasting for about 15 minutes, heat the stock in a saucepan until almost boiling, then turn the heat down, cover with a lid and leave to simmer.
3. Heat the remaining oil in a large, heavy-based saucepan over a medium heat. Add the onion and cook for 2–3 minutes until just starting to turn golden. Stir in the garlic and cook for about 30 seconds, then add the leeks and bacon. Lower the heat and continue cooking for a further 3–4 minutes until the bacon has cooked through and the leeks have softened.
4. Stir in the rice until it is well coated in oil, then add a ladle of the hot stock and stir until all the liquid has been absorbed. Continue adding and stirring in the hot stock for 18–20 minutes until the rice is soft but still has a slight bite and all the liquid has been absorbed.
5. Take the squash out of the oven and stir it carefully into the risotto. Season lightly with salt and pepper and serve with mixed salad leaves.

lamb tagine

PREPARATION TIME **10 MINUTES** COOKING TIME **1¾ HOURS**
ADDITIONAL TIME **MAKING THE STOCK AND THE RAS EL HANOUT** SERVES **4**

125ml/4fl oz/½ cup Vegetable Stock (see page 25), or stock made from gluten-, yeast- and dairy-free stock powder
¼ tsp saffron strands
3 tbsp olive oil
650g/1lb 7oz boneless shoulder of lamb, trimmed of fat and cut into bite-sized pieces
2 onions, finely chopped
2 garlic cloves, crushed
2 tbsp Ras el Hanout (see page 20)
200g/7oz sugar-free dried unsulphured apricots, cut in half
100g/3½oz/⅔ cups whole blanched almonds
3 tbsp clear honey

1 Heat the stock in a saucepan until almost boiling. Remove from the heat and stir in the saffron.
2 Heat 2 tbsp of the oil in a large, heavy-based saucepan over a medium heat. Add the lamb and cook for 3–4 minutes, stirring occasionally, until lightly browned. Remove the lamb from the pan using a slotted spoon and put in a bowl and drain off any juices into the bowl.
3 Heat the remaining oil in the pan over a medium heat. Add the onions and cook for 1–2 minutes until slightly softened. Stir in the garlic, then the ras el hanout and cook for about 30 seconds. Return the lamb and juices to the pan and add the apricots, almonds, honey and stock.
4 Bring to the boil, then turn the heat down, cover with a lid and leave to simmer for 1½ hours, stirring occasionally. Skim off any fat from the surface and serve with steamed rice and vegetables.

lamb skewers with pomegranate and yogurt sauce

PREPARATION TIME **10 MINUTES, PLUS 30 MINUTES MARINATING TIME**
COOKING TIME **8–12 MINUTES** SERVES **4**

500g/1lb 2oz lamb fillet, trimmed of fat and cut into bite-sized pieces
3 peppers (a mixture of red, orange and yellow, or all one colour), deseeded and cut into large chunks
8 shallots, peeled and cut in half lengthways
200g/7oz closed-cup mushrooms
200g/7oz cherry tomatoes
150ml/5fl oz/scant 2/3 cup olive oil

Sauce:
1 pomegranate
300g/10oz soya yogurt
1 1/2 tbsp finely chopped mint leaves
sea salt

1 Put the lamb in a large, flat, non-metallic dish and season lightly with salt. Add the peppers, shallots, mushrooms and tomatoes and pour the oil over them. Cover and leave to marinate for at least 30 minutes while soaking eight wooden skewers in water.
2 Preheat the grill to high. Thread the lamb and vegetables onto the skewers, alternating each ingredient. Place on the grill rack and cook under the hot grill for 4–6 minutes on each side until the lamb is crisp and brown on the outside but still pink in the middle.
3 Meanwhile, halve the pomegranate and, holding each half over a large bowl, bash the outer skin with a wooden spoon until all the seeds fall out into the bowl. You'll need to bash the skin a few times before the pips begin to fall out, but they will. Mix in the yogurt and mint and season lightly with salt. Serve the skewers with the sauce and steamed rice.

beef stroganoff

PREPARATION TIME **5 MINUTES** COOKING TIME **12–20 MINUTES** SERVES **4**

25g/1oz dairy-free margarine
2 small red onions, finely chopped
1–1½ tsp paprika
350g/12oz closed-cup mushrooms, sliced
600g/1lb 5oz fillet steak, cut into strips
3 tbsp olive oil
400g/14oz soya yogurt
1 large handful flat-leaf parsley, finely chopped
sea salt and freshly ground black pepper

1. Melt the margarine in a large, heavy-based saucepan. Add the onions and 1 tsp paprika and cook over a medium heat for 2–3 minutes until starting to turn golden. Stir in the mushrooms and cook for 5–7 minutes. Tip the onions and mushrooms onto a plate.
2. Season the steak lightly with salt and pepper. Heat 2 tbsp of the oil in the saucepan over a high heat. Add half the seasoned steak and cook for 2–4 minutes, turning, until browned. Remove from the pan using a slotted spoon and leave to one side. Repeat with the remaining oil and steak.
3. Return the onions and mushrooms to the pan. Using a whisk or a hand-held electric blender, blend the yogurt until smooth. Stir the yogurt into the mixture and heat through gently for 1–2 minutes, taking care not to overcook, as the yogurt will curdle. Stir in the steak and parsley, then check the seasoning and add more paprika if required. Serve with steamed rice and vegetables.

spaghetti with meatballs

PREPARATION TIME **10 MINUTES** COOKING TIME **20–25 MINUTES**
ADDITIONAL TIME **MAKING THE SAUCE** SERVES **4**

3 tbsp olive oil
1 onion, finely chopped
1 garlic clove, crushed
600g/1lb 6oz minced steak
1 egg, beaten
1 large handful flat-leaf parsley, finely chopped
400g/14oz gluten-free spaghetti, or other gluten-free pasta shape
1 recipe quantity Tomato and Pepper Sauce (see page 18)
sea salt and freshly ground black pepper

1 Heat 1 tbsp of the oil in a large, heavy-based frying pan. Add the onion and cook over a medium heat for 2–3 minutes until turning golden. Add the garlic and cook for 30 seconds.
2 Tip the onion and garlic into a large mixing bowl. Add the minced steak, egg and parsley and season lightly with salt and pepper. Mix well to combine the ingredients, then divide the mixture into 16 pieces and shape each into a ball with your hands.
3 Heat the tomato and pepper sauce in a large, heavy-based saucepan over a gentle heat until almost boiling.
4 Heat another 1 tbsp of the oil in the frying pan. Add half the meatballs and cook over a medium heat for 8–10 minutes, moving them around the pan so that they brown evenly and are cooked through. Remove from the frying pan with a slotted spoon and add to the saucepan with the tomato and pepper sauce. Repeat with the remaining meatballs.
5 Meanwhile, bring a large saucepan of water to the boil. Add the remaining oil, then the spaghetti, pushing it down into the water as it softens. Cook over a medium heat for 8–10 minutes, or according to the packet instructions, stirring frequently to make sure the spaghetti does not stick together. Drain, then rinse well with boiling water and drain again. Serve with the meatballs in the tomato and pepper sauce and with mixed salad leaves.

steak with baked asparagus and hollandaise sauce

PREPARATION TIME **5 MINUTES** COOKING TIME **10–12 MINUTES**
ADDITIONAL TIME **MAKING THE SAUCE** SERVES **4**

500g/1lb 2oz asparagus, woody ends removed

2½ tbsp olive oil

4 fillet steaks

1 recipe quantity Hollandaise Sauce (see page 19)

sea salt and freshly ground black pepper

1 Preheat the oven to 180°C/350°F/Gas 4. Place the asparagus on a baking tray. Drizzle with 1½ tbsp of the oil and bake in the hot oven for 10–12 minutes until cooked through.
2 Meanwhile, heat the remaining oil in a large, heavy-based frying pan. Season the steaks lightly with salt and pepper, add to the pan and cook over a medium heat for 3–5 minutes on each side for medium-rare or another 1–2 minutes for well done. Alternatively, brush the steaks with the remaining oil and cook under a hot grill.
3 Take the asparagus out of the oven and serve with the steak and the hot hollandaise sauce, and with boiled new potatoes or jacket potatoes.

ginger chilli tuna

PREPARATION TIME **10 MINUTES, PLUS 1 HOUR MARINATING TIME**
COOKING TIME **6–8 MINUTES** SERVES **4**

4 tuna steaks

1 tbsp olive oil

Marinade:

2cm/¾in piece fresh ginger, peeled and finely chopped

2 large garlic cloves, finely chopped

1 small or ½ large red chilli, deseeded and finely chopped

2 heaped tbsp chopped mint leaves

2 heaped tbsp chopped basil leaves

1 handful coriander leaves, finely chopped

3 tbsp olive oil

1 tbsp Thai fish sauce

juice of 2 limes

1. Place the tuna in a shallow, non-metallic dish. Mix together all the marinade ingredients in a bowl or jug and pour over the tuna. Cover with a lid or cling film and leave to marinate in the fridge for at least 1 hour, preferably longer.
2. Heat the oil in a heavy-based frying pan over a medium heat. Place the tuna in the hot pan, spoon the marinade on top of each steak and pour the remaining liquid into the base of the pan. Cook for 3–4 minutes on each side until the tuna is lightly browned on the outside but remains slightly pink in the centre. Serve with Vegetable Stir-fry (see page 146).

salmon with honey and ginger

PREPARATION TIME **5 MINUTES, PLUS 1 HOUR MARINATING TIME**
COOKING TIME **30–35 MINUTES** SERVES **4**

4 salmon fillets
2.5cm/1in piece fresh ginger, peeled and finely chopped
1 bunch spring onions, finely chopped
2 tbsp tamari soy sauce
2 tbsp clear honey

1. Place the salmon fillets in a large ovenproof dish, skin-side down. Sprinkle the ginger and spring onions over the top, then pour the tamari soy sauce and honey over. Cover with a lid and leave to marinate in the fridge for at least 1 hour, preferably longer.
2. Preheat the oven to 180°C/350°F/Gas 4. Place the dish in the hot oven and cook for 30–35 minutes until the salmon is cooked through.
3. Take the salmon fillets out of the oven and serve with the sauce from the dish and steamed rice or Herb Mash (see page 141) and vegetables.

salmon fishcakes

PREPARATION TIME **15 MINUTES, PLUS 30 MINUTES CHILLING TIME**
COOKING TIME **35–45 MINUTES** SERVES **4**

500g/1lb 2oz salmon fillets
2 tbsp olive oil
500g/1lb 2oz potatoes, peeled and cut into large chunks
2 large eggs, beaten
gram flour, for dusting
polenta or maize flour, for dusting
sea salt and freshly ground black pepper

1 Preheat the oven to 180°C/350°F/Gas 4. Place the salmon in an ovenproof dish and drizzle over half of the oil. Cover and bake in the hot oven for 20–25 minutes until cooked through.
2 Meanwhile, put the potatoes in a saucepan and cover with cold water. Place over a high heat, bring to the boil, then turn the heat down, cover with a lid and leave to simmer for 15–20 minutes until tender. Drain, return to the saucepan and heat gently for 1–2 minutes to dry out. Mash coarsely.
3 Take the salmon out of the oven, remove and discard the skin and any brown meat, and flake with a fork, reserving any juices. Mix together the flaked salmon, mashed potatoes, half the beaten eggs, the reserved cooking juices and some salt and pepper, taking care not to break up the fish too much. With wet hands, shape the salmon mixture into eight balls, then flatten them slightly to form fishcakes.
4 Spread the gram flour out on a plate and the polenta or maize flour out on a second plate. Dip each fishcake into the gram flour to coat it, then into the remaining beaten egg, then finally into the polenta or maize flour until well coated. Place on a clean plate, cover with cling film and leave to chill in the fridge for at least 30 minutes.
5 Heat the remaining oil in a large, heavy-based frying pan over a medium heat. Add half the fishcakes and cook for 4–5 minutes on each side until golden brown. Keep warm while you cook the remaining fishcakes. Serve with vegetables or mixed salad leaves.

herbed monkfish wrapped in parma ham

PREPARATION TIME **10 MINUTES, PLUS 2 HOURS CHILLING TIME** COOKING TIME **12–16 MINUTES** SERVES **4**

600g/1lb 5oz monkfish fillet, cut lengthways into four long pieces
1 large handful chopped coriander leaves
1 large handful chopped flat-leaf parsley
juice of 1 lemon
6 tbsp olive oil
8 slices nitrate-free Parma ham
sea salt and freshly ground black pepper

1 Place the monkfish pieces in a shallow, non-metallic dish. Mix together the coriander, parsley, lemon juice and oil in a jug and season lightly with salt and pepper. Pour over the fish, cover the dish and leave to marinate in the fridge for at least 2 hours.
2 Preheat the grill to high. Place two slices of Parma ham, side by side, on a clean surface. Remove one piece of monkfish from the dish, making sure that it is well coated in chopped herbs from the marinade, and lay it across the slices of ham. Carefully roll the ham around the herbed fish. Repeat with the remaining pieces of fish and ham.
3 Arrange the ham-wrapped pieces of fish on the grill rack and cook under the hot grill for 6–8 minutes on each side until the fish is cooked. Serve with boiled new potatoes and Italian-style Vegetables (see page 148).

baked sea bass with tarragon sauce and fennel purée

PREPARATION TIME **15 MINUTES** COOKING TIME **1 HOUR** ADDITIONAL TIME **MAKING THE STOCKS** SERVES **4**

3 tbsp olive oil
3 shallots, finely chopped
375ml/13fl oz/1½ cups organic dry white wine
500ml/17fl oz/2 cups Fish Stock (see page 25), or vegetable stock made from gluten-, yeast- and dairy-free stock powder
12 tarragon sprigs
2 large or 4 medium sea bass, gutted and cleaned
1 tbsp cornflour
150ml/5fl oz/scant ⅔ cup sugar-free soya milk
30g/1¼oz silken tofu

Fennel purée:
2 fennel bulbs, trimmed and sliced lengthways
175ml/6fl oz/¾ cup Vegetable Stock (see page 25), or stock made as before
sea salt and freshly ground black pepper

1 Preheat the oven to 180°C/350°F/Gas 4. Heat 2 tbsp of the oil in a large, heavy-based saucepan over a medium heat. Add the shallots and cook for 1–2 minutes until starting to turn golden. Add the wine, bring to the boil, then turn the heat down and leave to simmer for 15–20 minutes until the liquid has reduced. Add the fish stock, return to the boil, then turn the heat down and leave to simmer for a further 20 minutes.
2 Meanwhile, place the fennel and vegetable stock in a saucepan and bring to the boil. Lower the heat, cover with a lid and simmer for 10 minutes until the fennel is soft. Using a hand-held electric blender, blend to form a smooth purée. Alternatively, blend in a liquidizer or food processor. Season lightly with salt and pepper and keep warm.
3 Divide eight of the tarragon sprigs between the cavities in the fish. Place the fish in an ovenproof dish, drizzle over the remaining oil and bake in the hot oven for 20–30 minutes until cooked through.
4 Mix 1 tbsp water and the cornflour in a bowl to form a smooth paste. Add the milk and tofu and, using a hand-held blender, blend the mixture until smooth. Pour into the stock mixture, turn the heat up and bring the sauce to the boil, stirring constantly. Turn the heat down and leave to simmer for 8–10 minutes until the sauce is thick enough to coat the back of a spoon. Chop the remaining tarragon finely and stir into the sauce.
5 Take the fish out of the oven and serve with the fennel purée, the tarragon sauce and boiled new potatoes.

salmon and prawn fish pie

PREPARATION TIME **10 MINUTES** COOKING TIME **50–60 MINUTES**
ADDITIONAL TIME **MAKING THE STOCK AND THE SAUCE** SERVES **4**

500g/1lb 2oz salmon fillets
1 bay leaf
700ml/1¼ pints/scant 3 cups Fish Stock (see page 25), or vegetable stock made from gluten-, yeast- and dairy-free stock powder
1kg/2lb 4oz potatoes, peeled and cut into large chunks
4 tbsp sugar-free soya milk
1 egg, beaten
50g/2oz dairy-free margarine
250g/9oz cooked, peeled king prawns, deveined
1 recipe quantity Béchamel Sauce (see page 18)
sea salt and freshly ground black pepper

1 Place the salmon in a large, heavy-based saucepan, add the bay leaf and fish stock and bring to the boil over a medium heat. Turn the heat down, cover with a lid and leave to simmer for 8 minutes until the fish is cooked through. Remove from the pan using a slotted spoon and leave to cool. Reserve the cooking liquid.

2 Meanwhile, preheat the oven to 200°C/400°F/Gas 6. Put the potatoes in a large saucepan and cover with cold water. Place over a high heat, bring to the boil, then turn the heat down, cover with a lid and leave to simmer for 15–20 minutes until tender. Drain, stir in 4 tbsp of the reserved fish cooking liquid, the soya milk, egg and margarine and season lightly with salt and pepper. Mash until well blended and smooth, using a hand-held electric blender if you want a very smooth result.

3 When the salmon has cooled enough to handle, remove and discard the skin and any brown meat. Break into large, bite-sized chunks and arrange in the bottom of a 2.5-litre/4-pint/10-cup ovenproof dish. Place the prawns on top and pour the béchamel sauce over to cover the fish.

4 Spoon the mashed potato over, spreading it evenly. Bake in the hot oven for 35–40 minutes until the top is golden, then take it out of the oven and serve with vegetables.

moules marinière

PREPARATION TIME **15 MINUTES** COOKING TIME **5–7 MINUTES** SERVES **4**

2kg/4lb 8oz fresh mussels in their shells
50g/2oz dairy-free margarine
2 small onions, finely chopped
1 garlic clove, finely chopped
250ml/9fl oz/1 cup organic dry white wine
60g/2¹/₄oz soya yogurt
1 large handful chopped flat-leaf parsley
sea salt and freshly ground black pepper

1. Scrub the mussels thoroughly with a stiff brush under cold running water to remove all traces of grit, then remove any barnacles or other debris attached to the shells and pull off and discard the "beard" of fibrous material around the edge. Rinse again and discard any mussels that are open.
2. Melt the margarine in a large, heavy-based saucepan over a medium heat. Add the onions and cook for 2–3 minutes until they start to turn golden. Stir in the garlic and cook for 30 seconds.
3. Add the mussels and wine, turn up the heat a little, cover with a lid and cook for 3–4 minutes until the mussels have opened. Discard any that do not open.
4. Using a whisk or a hand-held electric blender, blend the yogurt until smooth. Stir the yogurt and chopped parsley into the wine and season lightly with salt and pepper. Heat through briefly, taking care not to overheat, or the yogurt will curdle. Serve with chunks of bread (see pages 23–4) and mixed salad leaves.

grilled prawns with mango salsa

PREPARATION TIME **15 MINUTES, PLUS 1 HOUR MARINATING TIME** COOKING TIME **8–11 MINUTES** SERVES **4**

750g/1lb 9oz raw, peeled, large king prawns, tails attached, deveined
6 spring onions, finely sliced
2cm/¾in piece fresh ginger, peeled and finely chopped
2 garlic cloves, finely chopped
½ large red chilli, deseeded and very finely chopped
1 large handful chopped coriander leaves
juice of 2 limes
4 tbsp olive oil
300g/10oz rice noodles

Mango salsa:
2 large ripe mangoes
6 spring onions, finely sliced
1 large red chilli, deseeded and very finely chopped
1 large handful chopped coriander leaves
juice of 2 limes

1 Place the prawns in a shallow, non-metallic dish and sprinkle the spring onions, ginger, garlic, chilli, coriander, lime juice and oil over the top. Mix to combine, cover the bowl with a lid or cling film and leave in the fridge to marinate for at least 1 hour, preferably longer.

2 Meanwhile, prepare the salsa. With a sharp knife, carefully slice the mango down the sides, avoiding the stone. Cut the flesh inside the slices into small squares, cutting down to the peel but not piercing it, and scoop out with a spoon. Peel the remains of the mango, slice the flesh from the stone and place all the flesh in a mixing bowl. Add the spring onions, chilli, coriander and lime juice and stir to mix well.

3 When the prawns have marinated, preheat the grill to high. Remove the prawns from the marinade and arrange on a rack over a grill pan. Pour the marinade mixture through a sieve into a large saucepan and discard the pulp. Stir in the rice noodles and pour over enough boiling water to cover. Place over a medium heat and cook for 4–5 minutes until the noodles are soft. Drain and keep warm.

4 Cook the prawns under the hot grill for 2–3 minutes on each side until pink and firm. Serve with the noodles and a helping of mango salsa.

rice paper rolls with mint and prawns

PREPARATION TIME **45 MINUTES** SERVES **4**

60g/2½oz rice vermicelli
16 rice paper sheets
1 bunch mint, leaves only
64 cooked, peeled, small king prawns, deveined, about 400g/14oz total weight
2 carrots, peeled and cut into matchsticks
½ cucumber, cut into matchsticks
4 spring onions, white part only, sliced thinly lengthways then each part chopped into eight
tamari soy sauce, for dipping

1 Place the rice vermicelli in a large bowl, cover with boiling water and leave to stand for 5–6 minutes until the vermicelli is soft. Rinse well under cold running water, then drain.
2 Refill the large bowl with fresh boiling water and place one rice paper sheet in it. Leave to stand for 30 seconds until the paper is soft. Fold a clean, damp tea towel in half, carefully remove the rice paper from the water and place it on top of the cloth.
3 Arrange 3–5 mint leaves, depending on size, horizontally on the paper, slightly off-centre towards you, leaving a gap on each side. Put 3–4 prawns on top, followed by 3–4 sticks of carrot, then 3–4 sticks of cucumber. Add a few slices of spring onion and cover with a little of the vermicelli.
4 Fold the side of the rice paper nearest to you over the stack of vegetables and prawns, making sure it is tight, then fold in the ends. Carefully roll the stack until all the rice paper is wrapped around it. Set aside on a plate, covered with a damp cloth, while you prepare the others. Repeat with the remaining sheets of rice paper, mint, prawns and vegetables, refreshing the boiling water whenever necessary. Serve the rolls with tamari soy sauce for dipping.

mushroom, spinach and egg stack

PREPARATION TIME **10–15 MINUTES** COOKING TIME **10–15 MINUTES**
ADDITIONAL TIME **MAKING THE POLENTA** SERVES **4**

4 tbsp olive oil
4 large, open mushrooms, about 400g/14oz total weight, stalks removed
3 large garlic cloves, finely chopped
400g/14oz closed-cup mushrooms, cut into quarters
400g/14oz baby leaf spinach
300g/10oz soya yogurt
4 large eggs
1 recipe quantity freshly cooked Quick Polenta, grilled or fried (see page 143)
sea salt and freshly ground black pepper

1 Heat 1 tbsp of the oil in a large, heavy-based saucepan over a medium heat. Add the large, open mushrooms, open-side up, and cook for 3–4 minutes until cooked through. Remove from the pan and keep warm.
2 Wipe the pan clean and heat the remaining oil in it over a medium heat. Add the garlic and cook for about 30 seconds. Add the closed-cup mushrooms and cook for 4–5 minutes, stirring continuously, then the spinach and cook for 2–3 minutes, stirring, until the spinach has wilted and some of the liquid has evaporated. Using a whisk or hand-held electric blender, blend the yogurt until smooth. Remove the vegetables from the heat, pour the yogurt into the pan and stir gently. Season lightly with salt and pepper, then cover to keep the mixture warm.
3 Meanwhile, bring a large saucepan of water to the boil, then lower the heat to a simmer. Stir the water vigorously, crack the eggs one at a time into a cup and, making sure the water is still swirling around, gently slip them into the water. Poach for 3–4 minutes until the whites are set but still soft and the yolks still runny.
4 Place one slice of grilled or fried polenta on each plate and put one large mushroom on top. Spoon a little of the warm spinach and mushroom mixture on top of the large mushrooms and place the rest around the sides, on the polenta. Remove the eggs from the pan with a slotted spoon, place one on top of each stack and serve.

chickpea and tomato stew

PREPARATION TIME **10 MINUTES, PLUS OVERNIGHT SOAKING TIME**
COOKING TIME **1½–2 HOURS** SERVES **4**

300g/12oz/1⅓ cups dried chickpeas, or 1½ x 410g/14oz tins salt-free chickpeas, drained and rinsed
1kg/2lb 4oz vine-ripened tomatoes
2 tbsp olive oil
1 onion, finely chopped
2 large garlic cloves, crushed
½ tsp sweet smoked paprika
¼ tsp paprika
½ tsp dried chilli flakes
200g/7oz soya yogurt
300g/12oz baby leaf spinach
sea salt and freshly ground black pepper

1 If using dried chickpeas, place them in a bowl, cover with cold water and leave to soak overnight or for at least 12 hours.
2 The next day, drain the chickpeas, then rinse thoroughly. Put in a large saucepan, cover with fresh water and bring to the boil. Boil rapidly for 10 minutes, then turn the heat down, cover with a lid and leave to simmer for 1–1½ hours until tender. Drain thoroughly.
3 With a sharp knife, cut a cross in the skin of each tomato, then place them in a large, heat-proof bowl and pour over enough boiling water to cover. Leave to stand for 2–3 minutes, then drain. Peel off and discard the skins, then chop each tomato into about eight pieces.
4 Heat the oil in a large, heavy-based saucepan over a gentle heat. Add the onion and cook for 2–3 minutes until golden in colour. Stir in the garlic, then the sweet smoked paprika, paprika and chilli flakes, and cook for 1–2 minutes, stirring continuously. Add the tomatoes, turn the heat up slightly and cook for 5 minutes, using the back of a wooden spoon to press down on the tomato pieces. Finally, add the cooked or tinned chickpeas and cook for 10–12 minutes until the sauce has reduced by about half.
5 Using a whisk or a hand-held electric blender, blend the yogurt until smooth. Stir into the mixture, turn the heat down and leave to simmer for a further 10 minutes until the chickpeas are tender, stirring occasionally. Season lightly with salt and pepper, then stir in the spinach and cook for about 1 minute until all the spinach has wilted and is well mixed in. Serve with steamed rice.

pasta puttanesca

PREPARATION TIME **10 MINUTES** COOKING TIME **20–25 MINUTES** SERVES **4**

1kg/2lb 4oz vine-ripened tomatoes
3 tbsp olive oil
4 garlic cloves, finely chopped
20 anchovies in oil, drained and chopped (optional)
4 tbsp capers in brine, rinsed
2 large red chillies, deseeded and finely chopped
2 handfuls chopped parsley
400g/14oz gluten-free penne, or other gluten-free pasta shape
sea salt and freshly ground black pepper

1 Cut a cross in the skin of each tomato and place in a large heatproof bowl. Pour over boiling water to cover and leave to stand for 2–3 minutes. Take the tomatoes out of the water and peel off and discard the skins. Chop each tomato into eight pieces.
2 Heat 2 tbsp of the oil in a heavy-based saucepan. Add the garlic, and anchovies if using, and cook over a low heat for 1 minute. Add the tomatoes, bring to the boil, then turn the heat down and simmer for 15–20 minutes until the sauce has reduced and thickened.
3 Stir the capers and chillies into the tomato sauce and cook over a low heat for 4–5 minutes. Stir the chopped parsley through the sauce, season lightly with salt and pepper and cook for 1 minute.
4 Meanwhile, bring a large saucepan of water to the boil. Add the remaining oil, then the pasta. Cook over a medium heat for about 8–10 minutes, or according to the packet instructions, stirring frequently so that the pasta does not stick together. Drain and rinse well with boiling water, then drain again. Serve with the sauce and mixed salad leaves.

pasta primavera

PREPARATION TIME **12–15 MINUTES** COOKING TIME **11–14 MINUTES**
ADDITIONAL TIME **MAKING THE STOCK** SERVES **4**

650g/1lb 7oz peas in their pods, shelled (250g/9oz/1$^{2}/_{3}$ cups shelled)
400g/14oz asparagus, woody ends removed, cut into thirds
200g/7oz fine green beans, trimmed and cut in half
2 tbsp olive oil
400g/14oz gluten-free pasta
450g/1lb soya yogurt
5 tbsp organic dry white wine
5 tbsp Vegetable Stock (see page 25), or stock made from gluten-, yeast- and dairy-free stock powder
1 onion, finely chopped
2 garlic cloves, crushed
75g/2$^{1}/_{2}$oz rocket, coarsely chopped
1$^{1}/_{2}$ heaped tbsp chopped mint leaves
1$^{1}/_{2}$ heaped tbsp chopped flat-leaf parsley
sea salt and freshly ground black pepper

1. Place the peas, asparagus and beans in a steamer and cook over a medium heat for 3–4 minutes until just tender but still slightly crunchy. Drain.
2. Bring a large saucepan of water to the boil. Add 1 tbsp of the oil, then the pasta. Cook over a medium heat for about 8–10 minutes, or according to the packet instructions, stirring frequently so that the pasta does not stick together.
3. Meanwhile, spoon the yogurt into a bowl, then, using a whisk or hand-held electric blender, blend until smooth. Add the wine and stock and blend. Season lightly with salt and pepper.
4. Heat the remaining oil in a large, heavy-based saucepan. Add the onion and cook over a medium heat for 2–3 minutes until starting to turn golden. Stir in the garlic, then pour in the yogurt mixture, lower the heat and cook gently for 1 minute. Stir in the cooked vegetables and then the rocket, mint and parsley and cook for 1 minute to heat through, taking care not to cook for too long, or the yogurt will curdle.
5. Drain the pasta and rinse well with boiling water, then drain again. Serve with the sauce and mixed salad leaves.

roasted vegetable tarts

PREPARATION TIME **20 MINUTES** COOKING TIME **65–75 MINUTES**
ADDITIONAL TIME **MAKING THE PASTRY** MAKES **4 OR 6**

3 peppers (a mixture of red, orange and yellow or all one colour), deseeded and cut into quarters
3 tbsp olive oil
3 large vine-ripened tomatoes, each cut into 8 pieces
1 onion, cut into 16 pieces
dairy-free margarine, for greasing
1 recipe quantity Rich Shortcrust Pastry, or gluten-free version (see page 21)
rice flour, for dusting
2 large eggs plus 6 large egg yolks, beaten
4 tbsp sugar-free soya milk
sea salt and freshly ground black pepper

1 Preheat the oven to 180°C/350°F/Gas 4. Arrange the peppers, cut-side down, and the tomatoes and onions on two baking trays and drizzle over the oil. Place both trays of vegetables in the hot oven and roast for about 20–25 minutes. Remove the tomatoes and onions, but leave the peppers to roast for a further 10 minutes until the skins are black.
2 Put the peppers in a plastic food bag and leave for 2–3 minutes. Remove from the bag and peel off the skins. Turn the oven up to 200°C/400°F/Gas 6. Grease 1½ x four-hole Yorkshire pudding tins or 6 x 12cm/5in tartlet tins, 2cm/¾in deep, with dairy-free margarine.
3 Gently roll out the pastry on a surface liberally dusted with rice flour until about 2mm/⅛in thick. Using a pastry cutter that is slightly larger in diameter than the Yorkshire pudding tin holes or the tartlet tins, to allow enough pastry for the sides, cut out six or four pastry circles, discarding any extra pastry. Be very gentle, as the dough will still be slightly sticky.
4 Lift the pastry circles into each hole (you may need to use a metal spatula) and press down lightly to remove any pockets of air. Line each pastry case with a piece of non-stick baking parchment and fill with baking beans. Place the tartlet tins, if using, on a baking tray. Bake in the hot oven for 8–10 minutes until firm and lightly golden. Take the pastry cases out of the oven and remove the parchment and beans.Turn the oven down to 180°C/350°F/Gas 4.
5 Divide the roasted onion between the pastry cases, then top each with four tomato pieces and two pepper quarters. Mix the eggs, egg yolks and soya milk together in a bowl and season lightly with salt and pepper. Pour the mixture over the vegetables.
6 Bake the filled pastry cases in the hot oven for 25–30 minutes until the filling is cooked through. Take them out of the oven, leave to cool in the tins until the filling has set, then carefully ease out onto a plate and serve with vegetables or mixed salad leaves.

sides

Fill your plate with the delicious side dishes featured in these pages. Creamy mashed potato with herbs or with olive oil is great with dishes such as Salmon with Honey and Ginger, for example, while the depth of the flavours in Potatoes with Porcini Mushrooms complements the Confit of Duck beautifully. Then there's Quick Polenta, which you can make in a matter of minutes and serve with strong tastes such as Chicken with Salsa Verde. Vegetables can make a meal spectacular – the combination of Vegetable Stir-fry with the Ginger Chilli Tuna, for example, adds variety and zing to the meal, while the addition of Italian-style Vegetables to the Herbed Monkfish Wrapped in Parma Ham brings out the complexity of tastes and textures. So, sign up for an organic box scheme and invest in a great peeler!

herb mash

PREPARATION TIME **5 MINUTES** COOKING TIME **15–20 MINUTES** SERVES **4**

800g/1lb 12oz potatoes, peeled and cut into large chunks
80g/2¾oz dairy-free margarine, diced
150ml/5fl oz/scant ⅔ cup sugar-free soya milk
1 bunch flat-leaf parsley or coriander
sea salt and freshly ground black pepper

1 Put the potatoes in a saucepan and cover with cold water. Place over a high heat, bring to the boil, then turn the heat down, cover with a lid and leave to simmer for 15–20 minutes until tender. Drain, then mash thoroughly until smooth. For very smooth mash, use a hand-held electric blender or a food processor.
2 Stir in the margarine with the milk and chopped parsley or coriander, then season lightly with salt and pepper and serve.

VARIATION

To make Olive Oil Herb Mash, follow the method above, substituting 3 tbsp olive oil for the dairy-free margarine.

potatoes with porcini mushrooms

PREPARATION TIME **10 MINUTES PLUS 30 MINUTES SOAKING TIME**
COOKING TIME **1¼–1½ HOURS** SERVES **4**

100g/3½oz dried porcini mushrooms, or dried mixed wild mushrooms
dairy-free margarine, for greasing
900g/2lb potatoes, peeled and thinly sliced
4 tbsp olive oil
sea salt and freshly ground black pepper

1 Place the mushrooms in a bowl, cover with boiling water and leave to stand for 30 minutes.
2 Preheat the oven to 180°C/350°F/Gas 4. Grease a large ovenproof dish with dairy-free margarine. Drain the mushrooms, reserving 150ml/5fl oz/scant ⅔ cup of the liquid.
3 Cover the base of the prepared dish with a layer of potato slices. Top with a layer of mushrooms and season lightly with salt and pepper. Repeat the layers until all the mushrooms and potatoes slices are used up, finishing with a layer of potato. Pour over the reserved liquid from the mushrooms, then drizzle the olive oil over the top.
4 Cover with a lid or wrap the dish with greaseproof paper, ensuring the paper ends are tucked under the dish, and bake in the hot oven for 45 minutes. Uncover and return to the oven for a further 30–40 minutes until the potatoes are tender and the top layer is brown and crispy. Take out of the oven and serve.

quick polenta

PREPARATION TIME **10 MINUTES** COOKING TIME **5–16 MINUTES** SERVES **4**

225g/8oz quick-cook polenta

½ tsp dried chilli flakes (optional)

5–6 tbsp olive oil

sea salt and freshly ground black pepper

1 Pour 1 litre/1¾ pints/4 cups water into a large, heavy-based saucepan and bring to the boil. Lower the heat and pour the polenta in slowly, stirring all the while, then add the dried chilli flakes, if using. Cook gently for 5–6 minutes, stirring occasionally, until thick. Stir in 5 tbsp of the olive oil and remove from the heat. Season lightly with salt and pepper and either serve or spoon the mixture into a baking tray, smoothing it into a flat layer, and leave to stand for 5–10 minutes until set.

2 Cut the set polenta into four thick slices, then either cook under a hot grill for 2–3 minutes on each side until golden brown, or fry in 1 tbsp olive oil in a large, heavy-based frying pan over a medium heat for 4–5 minutes on each side until golden brown, and serve.

roasted vegetables

PREPARATION TIME **15 MINUTES** COOKING TIME **1½ HOURS** SERVES **4**

4 large sweet potatoes, peeled and cut into quarters
1 large butternut or other squash, peeled, deseeded and cut into same size pieces as the sweet potatoes
12 large carrots, peeled and cut into thin sticks
6 tbsp olive oil
2 garlic cloves, finely sliced
1 large red chilli, deseeded and finely chopped (optional)

1. Preheat the oven to 180°C/350°F/Gas 4.
2. Place all the vegetables in a large roasting tin. Drizzle the oil over them and toss well to coat, then sprinkle with the garlic, and the chilli if using.
3. Roast in the hot oven for 1½ hours, turning every half hour, until crisp and golden brown, then take the vegetables out of the oven and serve.

vegetable stir-fry

PREPARATION TIME **10 MINUTES** COOKING TIME **4–6 MINUTES** SERVES **4**

2 tbsp olive oil
1 bunch spring onions, finely sliced
2cm/¾in piece fresh ginger, peeled and finely chopped
½ large red chilli, deseeded and finely chopped
1 lemongrass stalk, finely chopped
2 large garlic cloves, finely chopped
250g/9oz fine green beans, cut into 5cm/2in lengths
200g/7oz sugar snap peas
300g/10oz pak choi, sliced into thirds widthways, stems and leaves separated
2 tbsp tamari soy sauce
1 heaped tbsp chopped mint leaves
1 heaped tbsp chopped basil leaves
1 large handful chopped coriander leaves

1. Heat a large wok over a medium-high heat until hot. Add the oil and swirl it around the wok. Stir in the spring onions, then the ginger, chilli, lemongrass and finally the garlic and stir-fry for 30 seconds. Add the beans and stir-fry for 1 minute.
2. Add the sugar snap peas and the pieces of pak choi stem. Pour in the tamari soy sauce and 4 tbsp water. Stir thoroughly and cook for 1–2 minutes. Add the pak choi leaves and cook for 1–2 minutes until all the vegetables are cooked but remain slightly crunchy.
3. Remove from the heat, stir in the chopped herbs and serve.

red cabbage and apple

PREPARATION TIME **10 MINUTES** COOKING TIME **2½ HOURS** SERVES **4**

20g/¾oz dairy-free margarine, plus extra for greasing
1 red cabbage, about 750g/1lb 9oz, halved lengthways, core removed and leaves diced
400g/14oz apples, peeled, cored and diced
1 onion, finely chopped
1 garlic clove, finely chopped
1 tsp ground allspice
3 tbsp date syrup or clear honey
2 tbsp white wine vinegar
sea salt and freshly ground black pepper

1 Preheat the oven to 150°C/300°F/Gas 2. Grease a large ovenproof dish with dairy-free margarine.
2 Arrange about a third of the cabbage on the base of the prepared dish. Cover with about a third of the apples and a third of the chopped onion. Sprinkle over a pinch of the chopped garlic, about a third of the allspice and 1 tbsp of the date syrup or honey, then season lightly with salt and pepper. Repeat this layering twice.
3 Pour the vinegar over the ingredients and dot with pieces of the margarine. Cover with a lid and bake in the hot oven for 2½ hours, stirring every 30 minutes, until the cabbage is tender. Take out of the oven and serve.

italian-style vegetables

PREPARATION TIME **10 MINUTES** COOKING TIME **20–25 MINUTES**
ADDITIONAL TIME **MAKING THE STOCK** SERVES **4**

2 fennel bulbs
3 tbsp olive oil
3 garlic cloves, finely sliced
200g/7oz Savoy cabbage, tough stalks removed, leaves chopped
200g/7oz Swiss chard, or 100g/3½oz spring greens, tough stalks removed, leaves chopped
250ml/9fl oz/1 cup Chicken or Vegetable Stock (see pages 24–5), or vegetable stock made from gluten-, yeast- and dairy-free stock powder
150g/5oz nitrate-free pancetta, diced
300g/10oz baby leaf spinach
1 large handful chopped flat-leaf parsley
sea salt and freshly ground black pepper

1 Trim off and discard the leafy fronds at the top of the fennel, then remove and discard the outer leaves. Slice each bulb in half lengthways and then slice each half into quarters.
2 Heat 2 tbsp of the oil in a heavy-based saucepan over a low heat. Add the fennel, cover the pan with a lid and cook, stirring occasionally, for 5–6 minutes until the fennel is just starting to brown. Stir in the garlic and cook for 30 seconds, then add the Savoy cabbage and Swiss chard or spring greens and cook, covered, for 3 minutes.
3 Pour in the stock, turn up the heat and bring to the boil. Remove the lid, turn the heat down and leave to simmer for 10–12 minutes until most of the liquid has evaporated and the vegetables are tender.
4 Meanwhile, heat the remaining oil in a heavy-based frying pan. Add the pancetta and fry for 4–5 minutes until just crispy. Remove from the pan and drain on kitchen paper.
5 Add the spinach to the pan of vegetables and, gently pressing the leaves down with the back of a wooden spoon, cook for 2–3 minutes until wilted. Remove from the heat, stir in the chopped parsley and season lightly with salt and pepper. Stir in the crispy pancetta and serve, using a slotted spoon to drain the vegetables of any remaining liquid.

desserts

Creamy, crumbly, fruity, chocolatey, light and summery or rich and heavenly – whatever kind of dessert you're looking for, you'll find it here. Choose from an array of cakes and tarts, including Rich Chocolate Tart, baked desserts, such as Raspberry Soufflés, or quick treats, such as Mango and Pistachio Fool. There are family favourites, too, such as Coconut Rice Pudding, super-healthy options, like Fruit Kebabs with Raspberry Coulis, and utterly indulgent dishes, such as Almond Cake with Passionfruit Syrup or the meltingly delicious Chocolate Fondue with Fruit. Desserts burst with intoxicating scents, colours, textures and tastes and are usually far easier to make than they appear. Most of these can be cooking away while you eat your main course, or made in advance – so go for it!

flourless chocolate cake

PREPARATION TIME **10 MINUTES** COOKING TIME **25–30 MINUTES** SERVES **10**

110g/3¾oz dairy-free margarine, plus extra for greasing
225g/8oz dairy-free dark chocolate, with at least 70 per cent cocoa solids
6 eggs, separated
125g/4oz/¾ cup fruit sugar

Topping:
150g/5oz dairy-free dark chocolate, with at least 70 per cent cocoa solids
150g/5oz chestnut purée
30g/1oz fruit sugar
30g/1oz dairy-free margarine

1 Preheat the oven to 180°C/350°F/Gas 4. Lightly grease a deep 20cm/8in cake tin with dairy-free margarine and line the base with a circle of non-stick baking parchment.
2 Break the chocolate into small pieces and place in a large heatproof bowl. Rest the bowl over a pan of gently simmering water, making sure that the bottom of the bowl does not touch the water. Stir from time to time until the chocolate has melted. Add the margarine to the bowl and continue stirring occasionally until it is completely melted and mixed in with the chocolate. Remove from the heat.
3 Put the egg whites in a mixing bowl and whisk using a hand-held electric whisk until they form stiff peaks. Add the sugar and continue whisking until they form glossy peaks.
4 Lightly beat the egg yolks in another bowl, then stir into the melted chocolate mixture until well blended. With a large metal spoon, carefully fold in the whisked egg whites until they are thoroughly mixed in.
5 Pour the mixture into the prepared cake tin and bake in the hot oven for 25–30 minutes until risen and cooked around the sides but still slightly soft in the centre. Insert a skewer into the middle of the cake and if there is only a little of the cake mixture sticking to it, the cake is ready. Take the cake out of the oven and leave to cool in the tin for about 5 minutes, then transfer to a wire rack and leave to cool completely.
6 Meanwhile, prepare the topping. Melt the chocolate as above. Add the chestnut purée and sugar and stir well, then stir in the margarine until thoroughly blended. Remove from the heat, leave to cool and serve with slices of the cake.

almond cake with passionfruit syrup

PREPARATION TIME **10 MINUTES** COOKING TIME **20–25 MINUTES** SERVES **6**

dairy-free margarine, for greasing
4 eggs plus 6 egg yolks
1/2 tsp ground cinnamon
100g/3½oz/heaped 1/2 cup fruit sugar
250g/9oz/2 1/2 cups ground almonds
100ml/3 1/2fl oz/scant 1/2 cup apple or mango juice

Passionfruit syrup:
10 passionfruits
125ml/4fl oz/1/2 cup apple or mango juice
6 tbsp fruit sugar

1. Preheat the oven to 180°C/350°F/Gas 4. Lightly grease a deep 20cm/8in cake tin with dairy-free margarine and line the base with a circle of non-stick baking parchment.
2. Put the eggs and egg yolks in a large mixing bowl with the cinnamon and sugar. Using a hand-held electric whisk, whisk until the mixture is very thick and creamy and has doubled in volume. When the whisk is lifted from the mixture, it should leave a ribbon-like trail. Fold in the ground almonds carefully, using a metal spoon, then stir in the apple or mango juice until evenly mixed.
3. Tip the mixture into the prepared cake tin and cook in the hot oven for 20–25 minutes until it is golden and well risen and a metal skewer inserted into the middle comes out clean. Take the cake out of the oven, turn out onto a wire rack and leave to cool a little.
4. Meanwhile, prepare the passionfruit syrup. Cut the passionfruits in half and scoop the seeds and pulp out into a heavy-based saucepan, discarding the skins. Stir in the apple or mango juice and the fruit sugar. Bring to the boil, then turn the heat down and leave to simmer for 20 minutes until the liquid has reduced by half. Leave to cool a little.
5. While the cake is still warm, spread the warm passionfruit syrup over the top and serve.

cherry tart

PREPARATION TIME **15 MINUTES** COOKING TIME **35–45 MINUTES**
ADDITIONAL TIME **MAKING THE PASTRY** SERVES **6–8**

80g/2$^{3}/_{4}$oz dairy-free margarine, plus extra for greasing
1 recipe quantity Sweet Rich Shortcrust Pastry (see page 21)
rice flour, for dusting
50g/2oz silken tofu
4 tbsp soya milk
50g/2oz/$^{1}/_{3}$ cup fruit sugar
1 tsp vanilla extract
4 egg yolks
350g/12oz cherries, pitted and halved

1 Preheat the oven to 200°C/400°F/Gas 6. Grease a 25cm/10in tart tin, 3cm/1$^{1}/_{4}$in deep, with dairy-free margarine.

2 Roll out the pastry on a pastry board liberally dusted with rice flour into a round about 2mm/$^{1}/_{8}$in thick and 3cm/1$^{1}/_{4}$in larger all around than the tin, to allow enough pastry for the sides. Be careful, as the pastry will still be slightly sticky. Place the tin face down on top of the pastry and trim round to neaten it, then turn the board over to drop it into the tin. Ease the pastry into place, pressing down carefully to remove any air pockets.

3 Line the pastry case with a piece of non-stick baking parchment and cover with baking beans. Bake in the hot oven for 10–12 minutes until just golden. Take the pastry case out of the oven and remove the parchment and beans. Turn the oven down to 180°C/350°F/Gas 4.

4 Meanwhile, prepare the filling. Using a hand-held electric blender or liquidizer, blend the tofu and soya milk together until smooth. Whisk the margarine and sugar together in a mixing bowl until light and fluffy. Beat in the vanilla extract and egg yolks, then pour in the tofu and soya milk mixture and beat again until thoroughly blended.

5 Arrange the cherries over the base of the pastry case and pour the filling mixture carefully over the top. Bake in the hot oven for 25–30 minutes until the top is golden brown. Take the tart out of the oven and leave to cool in the tin until the filling has set, then carefully ease it out onto a plate and serve.

tarte tatin

PREPARATION TIME **10 MINUTES** COOKING TIME **40–55 MINUTES**
ADDITIONAL TIME **MAKING THE PASTRY** SERVES **6**

75g/2½oz dairy-free margarine
100g/3½oz/heaped ½ cup fruit sugar
7 apples, peeled, cored and cut in half
1 recipe quantity Tarte Tatin Pastry (see page 22)
rice flour, for dusting

1 Heat the margarine gently in a 20cm/8in heavy-based frying pan with an ovenproof handle until melted. Sprinkle the sugar over the top, then arrange the apple halves, cut-side down, in one layer.
2 Cook over a gentle heat for 20–30 minutes until the apples are soft and golden and the liquid has caramelized. Remove from the heat.
3 Preheat the oven to 220°C/425°F/Gas 7. Roll the pastry out on a surface liberally dusted with rice flour into a round that is slightly larger than the frying pan. Be careful, as the pastry will still be slightly sticky. Trim the pastry neatly into a circle with a knife. Carefully lift the pastry with a metal spatula and place it on top of the pan, completely covering the apples.
4 Place the pan in the hot oven and bake for 20–25 minutes until the pastry is golden brown. Take the tart out of the oven and leave to cool in the pan for 2 minutes. Place a serving plate, upside-down, over the top of the pan, then, holding the pan and plate together, turn them over so that the tarte tatin turns out onto the serving plate with the caramelized apples on top, and serve.

rich chocolate tart

PREPARATION TIME **10 MINUTES** COOKING TIME **30–35 MINUTES**
ADDITIONAL TIME **MAKING THE PASTRY** SERVES **6–8**

60g/2¼oz dairy-free margarine, plus extra for greasing
1 recipe quantity Sweet Rich Shortcrust Pastry (see page 22)
rice flour, for dusting
200g/7oz dairy-free dark chocolate, with at least 70 per cent cocoa solids
50g/2oz silken tofu
80ml/2¾fl oz/⅓ cup soya milk
4 egg yolks
3 tbsp fruit sugar

1 Preheat the oven to 200°C/400°F/Gas 6. Grease a 25cm/10in tart tin, 3cm/1¼in deep, with dairy-free margarine.

2 Roll out the pastry on a pastry board liberally dusted with rice flour into a round about 2mm/⅛in thick and 3cm/1¼in larger all around than the tin, to allow enough pastry for the sides. Be careful, as the pastry will still be slightly sticky. Place the tin face down on top of the pastry and trim round to neaten it, then turn the board over to drop it into the tin. Ease the pastry into place, pressing down carefully to remove any air pockets.

3 Line the pastry case with a piece of non-stick baking parchment and cover with baking beans. Bake in the hot oven for 10-12 minutes until just golden. Take the pastry case out of the oven, remove the parchment and beans and turn the oven down to 180°C/350°F/Gas 4.

4 Meanwhile, prepare the chocolate filling. Break the chocolate into pieces and put in a heat-proof bowl, then rest the bowl over a saucepan of gently simmering water, making sure that the bottom of the bowl does not touch the water. Stir from time to time until the chocolate has melted. Remove the chocolate from the heat and stir in the margarine until melted. Using a hand-held electric blender or liquidizer, blend the tofu and soya milk until smooth.

5 Whisk the egg yolks in a large bowl, then add the sugar and whisk again until thick and creamy. Beat in the milk and tofu mixture until smooth, then stir in the melted chocolate and margarine and mix until well blended.

6 Pour the filling into the pastry case. Bake in the hot oven for 20–22 minutes until the filling is springy to the touch. Take the tart out of the oven and leave to cool in the tin until the filling has set. Ease it out onto a plate and serve.

coconut rice pudding

PREPARATION TIME **5 MINUTES** COOKING TIME **2 HOURS** SERVES **4**

dairy-free margarine, for greasing
800ml/1 pint 8fl oz/scant 3¼ cups coconut milk
200ml/7fl oz/¾ cup soya milk
100g/3½oz/scant ½ cup pudding rice
40g/1¾oz/¼ cup fruit sugar
3 dried star anise

1. Preheat the oven to 150°C/300°F/Gas 2. Lightly grease a 2.5-litre/4-pint/10-cup ovenproof dish with dairy-free margarine. Mix the milks together in a jug.
2. Put the rice in the prepared dish and mix in the sugar. Add the star anise, then pour the milk mixture over the top and stir. Bake in the warm oven for 2 hours, stirring every 30 minutes.
3. Take the pudding out of the oven. Using a large metal spoon, remove and discard the layer of coconut oil that will have formed on the top, then remove and discard the star anise before serving.

raspberry soufflés

PREPARATION TIME **10 MINUTES** COOKING TIME **12–17 MINUTES** SERVES **6**

dairy-free margarine, for greasing
5 egg whites
100g/3½oz/heaped ½ cup fruit sugar
300g/10oz raspberries
2 drops rosewater
1 tsp cornflour

1. Preheat the oven to 180°C/350°F/Gas 4. Grease six large, deep 350ml/12fl oz/scant 1½-cup ramekins or a 2-litre/3½-pint/8-cup soufflé dish with dairy-free margarine.
2. In a clean bowl, whisk the egg whites using a hand-held electric whisk until they form stiff peaks. Add half the sugar and continue whisking until they form glossy peaks.
3. Place the raspberries and the remaining sugar in a small, heavy-based saucepan and heat gently over a low heat for 4–5 minutes until the fruit has softened. Stir in the rosewater, then strain the mixture through a non-metallic sieve into a large mixing bowl. Mix 1 tsp water and the cornflour together in a small bowl to make a smooth paste and whisk into the strained raspberry mixture.
4. Add a third of the whisked egg whites to the raspberry mixture and whisk until well blended. With a metal spoon, carefully fold in the remaining egg whites until they are all thoroughly mixed in.
5. Pour the mixture into the prepared ramekins or soufflé dish and bake in the hot oven for 8–12 minutes, depending on the size, until very lightly browned on top and well risen. Take the soufflés out of the oven and serve immediately.

apricot clafoutis

PREPARATION TIME **10 MINUTES** COOKING TIME **65–70 MINUTES** SERVES **4**

dairy-free margarine, for greasing
800g/1lb 12oz ripe apricots, cut in half vertically and pitted
3 tbsp clear honey
4 eggs
100g/3½oz/heaped ½ cup fruit sugar
25g/1oz/2 heaped tbsp rice flour
25g/1oz/scant ¼ cup gram flour
500ml/17fl oz/2 cups soya milk

1 Preheat the oven to 180°C/350°F/Gas 4. Lightly grease a 2.5-litre/4-pint/10-cup ovenproof dish with dairy-free margarine.
2 Arrange the apricots cut-side up in a baking tray. Drizzle the honey into the hollow in the centres of the apricot halves and bake in the hot oven for 30 minutes.
3 Meanwhile, beat the eggs and sugar together in a mixing bowl with a hand-held electric whisk until thick and creamy. Sift in the flours and, with a metal spoon, carefully fold into the egg mixture. Stir in the soya milk, then place the batter in the fridge until the apricots are cooked.
4 Remove the cooked apricots from the oven and turn the temperature up to 190°C/375°F/Gas 5. Transfer the apricots to the prepared dish and pour over any honey remaining in the baking tray. Pour the batter over the top and bake in the hot oven for 35–40 minutes until well risen and set, with a golden-brown crust formed on the top. Take the clafoutis out of the oven and serve.

baked figs with yogurt and pine nuts

PREPARATION TIME **5 MINUTES** COOKING TIME **30–35 MINUTES** SERVES **4**

12 ripe figs

3 tbsp clear honey

80g/2¾oz/½ cup pine nuts

200g/7oz soya yogurt

1 Preheat the oven to 180°C/350°F/Gas 4. Place the figs in a large ovenproof dish and drizzle the honey over them. Bake in the hot oven for 30–35 minutes until the figs are tender and the juices have evaporated.

2 Meanwhile, heat a heavy-based frying pan over a medium heat. Toss in the pine nuts and dry-fry, stirring constantly, until just beginning to brown. Tip into a bowl.

3 When the figs are cooked, take them out of the oven and serve covered with yogurt and sprinkled with toasted pine nuts.

stuffed peaches

PREPARATION TIME **10 MINUTES** COOKING TIME **30–35 MINUTES** SERVES **4**

dairy-free margarine, for greasing
50g/2oz/scant 1/2 cup ground almonds
1 tbsp date syrup
1/2 tsp vanilla essence
4 large ripe peaches, cut in half vertically and pitted
185ml/6 1/2fl oz/2/3 cup organic dessert wine

1 Preheat the oven to 180°C/350°F/Gas 4. Lightly grease a large baking tin with dairy-free margarine.
2 Place the ground almonds, date syrup and vanilla essence in a mixing bowl and, using your fingers, rub the mixture together until well mixed. With a teaspoon, scoop a small circle of the flesh from the middle of each peach half, enlarging the hole left by the stone. Chop this flesh finely and stir into the almond mixture. Add 125ml/4 1/2fl oz/1/2 cup of the dessert wine and mix well.
3 Spoon 2 tsp of the almond mixture into the hole in the centre of each peach half. Place the peaches cut-side up in the prepared tin and bake in the hot oven for 30–35 minutes until golden brown.
4 Take the peaches out of the oven. Place two stuffed peach halves on each plate, pour 1 tbsp of the remaining dessert wine over them and serve.

baked strawberries with gooseberry custard

PREPARATION TIME **10 MINUTES** COOKING TIME **20–25 MINUTES** SERVES **4**

800g/1lb 12oz strawberries, hulled
500ml/17fl oz/2 cups soya milk
1 tbsp cornflour
5 large egg yolks
125g/4oz/heaped 2/3 cup fruit sugar
1/2 tsp vanilla extract
350g/12oz gooseberries, topped and tailed

1 Preheat the oven to 170°C/325°F/Gas 3. Place the strawberries on a large sheet of non-stick baking parchment on a baking tray, bring the sides together to make a parcel and tuck the ends under. Place in the hot oven and bake for 20–25 minutes until the fruit is starting to soften but still holds its shape.

2 Meanwhile, heat the soya milk in a heavy-based saucepan over a low heat until almost boiling. While the milk is warming, mix the cornflour and 1 tbsp water together in a small bowl to form a smooth paste. Whisk the egg yolks, 40g/1 3/4oz/ 1/4 cup of the fruit sugar and the cornflour paste together in a large mixing bowl until the mixture thickens. Pour in the hot millk and stir until thoroughly mixed.

3 Pour the mixture into a clean saucepan, add the vanilla extract and cook over a low heat for 10–15 minutes, stirring frequently, to form a thick custard. Be careful not to overheat or it may curdle; if it does, use a whisk or hand-held electric whisk to make it smooth again.

4 While the custard is cooking, put the gooseberries in a heavy-based saucepan with 1 tbsp water, bring to the boil, then turn the heat down and simmer for 5–10 minutes until soft, pushing the fruit down with a wooden spoon as it cooks. Using a hand-held electric blender, blend the fruit to form a smooth purée. Alternatively, blend the fruit in a liquidizer or food processor. Push through a sieve to remove the pips, discard the pulp and put in a clean bowl.

5 When the custard is cooked, stir it into the fruit purée along with the remaining sugar. Take the strawberries out of the oven and serve with the gooseberry custard.

fruit kebabs with raspberry coulis

PREPARATION TIME **10 MINUTES** COOKING TIME **12–15 MINUTES** SERVES **4**

8 apricots, cut in half and pitted
3 peaches or nectarines, peeled, cut in half and pitted, then each half cut into 4 pieces
1 pineapple
24 large strawberries, hulled

Raspberry coulis:
375g/13oz raspberries
35g/1½oz/scant ¼ cup fruit sugar

1. To make the coulis, place the raspberries and sugar in a heavy-based saucepan and cook gently over a low heat for 4–5 minutes. Push the mixture through a fine non-metallic sieve, discard the pulp and keep warm.
2. Place the apricots and peaches or nectarines in a large bowl. Trim the woody base and green top off the pineapple and, holding it upright, slice off and discard the skin, including the "eyes". Slice the flesh thickly lengthways, then remove and discard the core. Chop the flesh into bite-sized chunks. Add to the bowl of fruit with the strawberries.
3. Preheat the grill to high. Thread the fruit pieces onto eight long metal skewers, mixing the fruit pieces. Place on a grill rack under the hot grill and cook for 4–5 minutes on each side.
4. Serve the fruit skewers with the raspberry coulis.

mango and pistachio fool

PREPARATION TIME **5 MINUTES, PLUS 2 HOURS CHILLING TIME** SERVES **6**

4 tbsp cornflour
2 x 250ml/9fl oz/1-cup cartons or tins coconut cream
4 large ripe mangoes
60g/2¼oz/scant ½ cup shelled, unsalted pistachio nuts, finely chopped
2–3 tbsp clear honey

1 Add 3 tbsp water to the cornflour in a small bowl and stir to form a smooth paste. Put the coconut cream in a heavy-based saucepan and heat gently, adding the cornflour paste a little at a time and beating with a whisk throughout. Heat for 5–6 minutes until the mixture is thick, then whisk thoroughly and leave to cool.

2 With a sharp knife, carefully slice the mangoes down the sides, avoiding the stone. Cut the flesh inside the slices into small squares, cutting down to the peel but not piercing it, and scoop it out with a spoon. Peel the remaining parts of the mangoes and cut the flesh off the stones.

3 Put all the mango flesh and the coconut mixture in a bowl with half the pistachios and blend together thoroughly with a hand-held electric blender. Alternatively, blend them in a liquidizer or food processor. Add the honey to taste and blend quickly, then add the remaining pistachios, reserving 1 tbsp for later, and stir thoroughly.

4 Spoon the fool into glasses or bowls and leave to chill in the fridge for at least 2 hours. Sprinkle with the reserved pistachio nuts and serve.

chocolate fondue with fruit

PREPARATION TIME **10 MINUTES** COOKING TIME **10 MINUTES** SERVES **4**

1 pineapple
2 bananas, sliced into thick chunks
300g/10oz soft fruit, such as strawberries, hulled, and grapes
300g/10oz dairy-free dark chocolate, with at least 70 per cent cocoa solids
1½ tbsp blackstrap molasses or clear honey
2 cinnamon sticks

1 Trim the woody base and green top off the pineapple and, holding it upright, slice off and discard the skin, including the "eyes". Slice the flesh thickly lengthways, then remove and discard the core. Chop the flesh into bite-sized chunks and place in a large bowl along with the bananas and soft fruit. Toss gently to mix the fruit. Transfer to a serving dish.
2 Break the chocolate into small pieces and place in a heatproof bowl. Rest the bowl over a pan of barely simmering water, making sure that the bottom of the bowl does not touch the water. Stir from time to time until the chocolate has melted.
3 Stir the molasses or honey into the chocolate, then push the cinnamon sticks into the mixture, making sure they are covered. Leave to heat gently for 4–5 minutes. Remove the bowl from the heat and gradually stir in 100–120ml/3½–4fl oz/scant ½ cup water to form a thick chocolate cream. Remove and discard the cinnamon sticks. Serve the fondue with fruit for dipping.

chocolate and coconut mousse

PREPARATION TIME **10 MINUTES** COOKING TIME **10 MINUTES, PLUS 1 HOUR CHILLING TIME** SERVES **6**

2 tbsp cornflour
250ml/9fl oz/1-cup carton or tin coconut cream
200g/7oz dairy-free, dark chocolate, with at least 70 per cent cocoa solids
3 eggs, separated
unsweetened coconut flakes, to serve

1 Add $1^1/_2$ tbsp water to the cornflour in a small bowl and stir to form a smooth paste. Put the coconut cream in a heavy-based saucepan and heat gently, adding the cornflour paste a little at a time and beating with a whisk throughout. Heat for 5–6 minutes until the mixture is thick, then whisk thoroughly and leave to cool.
2 Break the chocolate into small pieces and place in a large heatproof bowl. Rest the bowl over a pan of gently simmering water, making sure that the bottom of the bowl does not touch the water. Stir from time to time until the chocolate has melted.
3 Add the egg yolks to the chocolate, whisk thoroughly using a hand-held electric whisk, then remove from the heat, add the coconut mixture and whisk thoroughly again.
4 Meanwhile, heat a heavy-based frying pan over a medium heat until hot. Add the coconut flakes and dry-fry until lightly browned, turning frequently to prevent burning. Tip the toasted flakes into a bowl.
5 Put the egg whites in a mixing bowl, clean the whisk, then whisk until they form stiff peaks. Using a metal spoon, fold the egg whites into the chocolate mixture, a third at a time, until they are all thoroughly mixed in.
6 Spoon into 6 × 175ml/6fl oz/$^3/_4$-cup ramekins and leave to chill in the fridge for at least 1 hour. Sprinkle with the toasted coconut flakes and serve.

index

a

b

c

d

e

f

g

h